THE ARISTOCRATS OF AUTO

THE UPPER CRUST

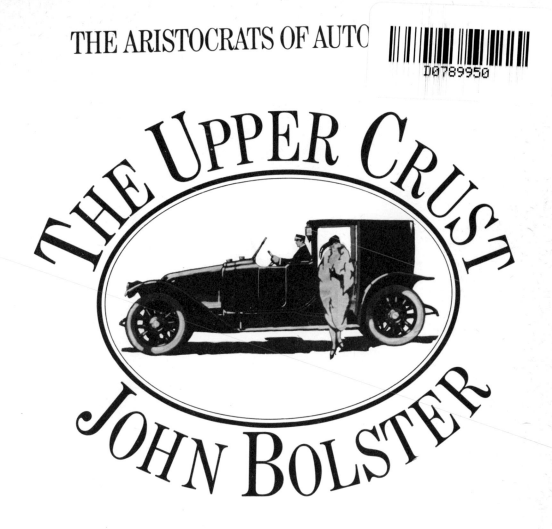

JOHN BOLSTER

FOLLETT PUBLISHING COMPANY
CHICAGO

Designed by Behram Kapadia
Printed in Great Britain

Library of Congress Catalogue Card No.: 74–31858
ISBN 0 695 80583 5

Contents

Foreword

There are those who insist that we are entering the twilight of the Motor Age.

The energy crisis, the cost of fuel and raw materials, sensitivity towards environmental considerations—all these have had world-wide repercussions on the automotive industry. That public attitudes towards the private car have changed dramatically and increasingly since the late sixties is demonstrable. Pedestrian precincts have grown apace in the cities of Europe. There is mounting antagonism towards the unbridled spread of motorways. Restrictive health and safety legislation has been introduced to popular acquiescence, if not acclaim.

And as for the manufacturers, who as little as three years ago would have dared predict that the latest advertising for high performance cars such as Lotus and BMW would be focused on fuel economy? That Porsche would be designing a car with a twenty-year life expectancy? That Volkswagen would be in serious financial difficulty, and that General Motors would embark on major research into hydrogen as an alternative fuel?

Twilight or not, few can doubt that motoring will never be quite the same again. We are overdue for a technological revolution in overland transport for which the world may or may not be a better place.

That being so, now may be as good a time as any to look back on the best of what has been. That is the purpose of this book.

The title was as self-evident as the choice of author – not that there is anything about John Bolster remotely associated with twilight or darkness.

It has been my pleasure to work with him, and count him amongst my friends, for more than 25 years. And since, if something once loved is passing, it is comforting to cherish its excellence, *The Upper Crust* had to be Bolster's book.

John Bolster's love affair with cars and driving has probably been the principal influence in his crowded life. And as is the way with love affairs, objectivity may not always have been its principal criterion.

Stories about John Bolster are told at the Steering Wheel Club in London, at Roger's in Paris, behind the pits at Le Mans and Sebring, at the International functions of the Guild of Motoring Writers, and many another good pull-up for car men. Most of those stories tend to be outrageously funny. All are told with affection.

When his tall, unmistakable figure, crowned always with a deer-stalker hat, was better known at the racing circuits than it is today, there may have been those tempted to dismiss him too lightly as 'a bit of a card'.

But his scholarly writing reveals an intellect capable, by all means, of donning cap and bells to delight his friends, but also of embracing that self-discipline which is essential as much to the historian as the great driver.

John Bolster designed, drove and named 'Bloody Mary' his immortal Shelsley Special, now in the National Motor Museum at Beaulieu. He made ERA racing cars go faster than they were ever intended, and had an accident in the process which would have killed a lesser man. He has written for years in technical French, as well as his native and beloved English. He has a considerable knowledge and taste for complex music, a profound admiration for the Prince Regent, and a charming country establishment where he keeps donkeys, and his agricultural equipment, as well as cars. John Bolster writes with dedication and authority on the subject nearest but one to his heart.

This is his book – written as much for the elderly lady remembering a more gracious age, as for her nephew, the knowledgeable young enthusiast.

It was my privilege to give him the opportunity to write it. It is my hope that its readers – whatever their particular interest in the subject – may share my delight in it.

RAYMOND BAXTER
May 1975

The Upper Crust

1
As it was in the Beginning

*T*his is really a tale of the road, that magic ribbon winding into the distance. At first it was a path, along which people walked or rode. Such goods and merchandise as had to be moved from place to place went on the backs of pack animals or were even carried by men. Their passage kept down the undergrowth as they twisted and turned between the trees, following the tracks of those that had gone before them.

The narrow path became the broad highway because of the wheel. Thereafter, for evermore, the quality of the highway was to dictate the design and construction of the vehicles that went upon it. The width of the first roads was that of 2 oxen, side by side, which were required to pull a reasonable load. This was also about the minimum width for a wheeled vehicle to be safe from overturning, when moving heavily laden over rough ground.

Too wide a road would be costly and laborious to build and so the standard track of all vehicles was settled incredibly early, for as roads began to be used, everybody must follow the same ruts. In every part of the world where the wheel was known, about the same width was chosen independently. The Romans built their roads of double width, about 14 ft, because they wanted chariots and wagons to meet and pass each other without stopping; their system of government demanded rapid communication by road.

Primitive roads were usually wider than this, to allow for going round patches of soft mud or deeply worn holes, but though the wheel will bear a far greater load than a beast of burden, it will carry many times more over a hard, smooth surface. The wheel needs the surface and the surface must have a foundation with proper drainage. These were the 2 things which the early dirt roads lacked and that the Romans brought to road-building.

Roman roads always had a deep stone foundation, though the surface might vary in different localities. It was often of paving stones – large or of the small, square type – cobbles, or even shingle. The road was generally raised and always cambered, for the Romans knew that the carriageway would become soft if water remained upon it. Similarly, they were careful to make channels beneath their roads to carry the smallest streams; it was the blocking of these culverts that caused stretches of Roman road to be ruined in the dark ages.

Mediaeval roads sometimes had drainage ditches alongside, but the Roman lesson of cambering had been forgotten. Travellers expected to have to repair the roads themselves as they went. They were generally quite well made in towns but in between were the meandering dirt roads of the country. The rolling English drunkard made the rolling English road, in sober truth.

Even the carriages of the upper crust were rough, clumsy vehicles, constructed to withstand being dragged out of swamps and ditches. Suspension springs to reduce the jolting were known in the seventeenth century, but they were seldom used because they might break under such treatment. When royalty travelled, they rode in state through the towns in their carriages, but out in the country they called for their horses, even the ladies of the court preferring to ride them, rather than submit to the jolting of the vehicles. No doubt there were those who were dreaming of mechanical propulsion in the future, but the roads of the middle ages would have been hopeless for anything of the kind.

In the eighteenth century, English major roads improved enormously and probably became better than those of any other country. This was due to the turnpike system, which was tried elsewhere but flourished especially in England. It was private enterprise at its best, men being permitted to take over sections of road, carry out all necessary repairs, and charge tolls for all the vehicles that passed.

There were those who considered the turnpikes an infringement of personal liberty. Riots took place and tollhouses were burnt down, but the system prospered and travel between the larger cities became quite easy and rapid. The turnpike system made the organization of efficient repair gangs possible, but their work became infinitely more effective when proper engineering principles were applied to road-building. The man who revolutionized the construction of roads was John Loudon Macadam, who lived from 1756 to 1836.

Macadam knew a lot about road foundations and quite a bit about drainage. He removed the top soil to a depth of 14 ins, replacing the first 7 ins with coarse, cracked stones. Any depressions were levelled and the interstices plugged with small, cracked stones. The upper 7 ins were filled with 'road metal', which means specially broken stones with no piece larger than $2\frac{1}{2}$ ins diameter. The surface was made by spreading stones crushed to dust, applying copious water, and rolling the resulting paste until it was smooth. Much later, this dust would prove an appalling nuisance when vehicles travelled more quickly.

Heaps of stones were kept at the roadside for repair and, labour being cheap, old men were permanently employed to break the road metal to the correct size, though it was a soul-destroying job. I can remember them sitting there, not so long ago, with their hammers and goggles for eye protection. They carried out temporary repairs to pot-holes, but, after a few years, a gang with a heavy roller would tear the top surface off the road and re-make it with the road metal from the ready-prepared heaps.

John Macadam's way of building roads became universal in Great Britain and spread to the Continent and the USA. With a small 'm', his name is used to denote either the surface of a road made on his principle or the broken stones for his road metal. It means the same in a French dictionary and the Germans render it as *Makadam*; he spelt it McAdam himself. Though the macadam became tarmacadam, or tarmac, on main roads in the early years of the present century, it was used in its original form for most minor roads until the 1930s in England and may still be found in many places.

Let us return to the lifetime of this immortal Scotsman, who refused a baronetcy but accepted a government grant of £10,000. His roads made the mechanically propelled vehicle possible and it

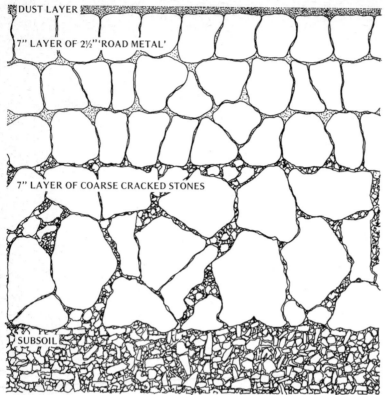

DUST LAYER

7" LAYER OF 2½"'ROAD METAL'

7" LAYER OF COARSE CRACKED STONES

SUBSOIL

Macadam roads made mechanical transport possible, but the water-bound surface rose in clouds of dust whenever a vehicle passed in the summer.

was not long before the steam engine was launched on the turnpikes. Already, full use was being made of these better roads by the stage-coaches. This was a highly competitive trade and though the speed was not high, remarkable journey times were achieved by extremely rapid changes of the team of 4 horses. The halts were as quick as a pit stop in a modern motor race and elaborate time-and-motion study was applied to the work of the coachman, grooms and ostlers.

Similarly, privately owned carriages no longer needed to be of tough construction to withstand falling into holes in the road. Lightly built, carried on slim wheels of great diameter, and softly suspended on long C-springs, they had a beauty which has never been surpassed. They became even more of a status symbol than a great house, as a man took his carriage wherever he went for all to see. Families owning them were referred to as carriage-folk and better-class shopkeepers were said to wait on the carriage-trade.

In addition to these luxurious conveyances, the young bloods drove the forerunners of the sports car. Very light 2-seater curricles, drawn by a pair of horses or even 4-in-hand, they were driven wildly, often for extravagant wagers, and kept the countryside in fear. Britain's Prince Regent was a notable exponent of these exercises.

All this buying of new horse-drawn vehicles by the rich caused a big expansion of the coachbuilding business. Great firms were founded that would be building superb car bodies several genera-tions later and the standard of craftsmanship was extremely high.

London probably led the world for quality, though there were those who admired the exquisite products of Paris.

All these magnificent machines relied on the horse for their motive power – the horse that grew tired all too soon, went lame with regrettable frequency, and ate you poor even when you were not using him. Great engines were running in the pumping stations, the mines, and the factories. Could not the wondrous power of steam be harnessed to a wheeled vehicle?

It proved comparatively easy to make a light and compact steam engine, but those huge stationary boilers, set in masonry, defied reproduction in a convenient size. It was the boiler, we are led to believe, which was the weak link in the famous *fardier* which Joseph Cugnot built for Napoleon. The first steam carriages would start off splendidly but could not maintain steam pressure. The problem was solved by creating a forced draught to make the fire burn more fiercely, first by using a rotary blower as on a threshing machine and then by directing the exhaust steam to cause a blast up the chimney.

The first successful constructor of steam carriages was Richard Trevithick, from 1801, and he actually made many runs through the streets of London in 1803. However, along with some other inventors, he transferred his allegiance to railways, as being more suitable for steam engines. Nevertheless, many people still believed in steam transport on the roads and a great many machines were built. These all tended to be too large and heavy for private use and were really enormous locomotives, carrying numerous paying passengers.

Many of these steam coaches failed because they literally shook themselves to pieces by travelling too fast. Wooden wheels with iron tyres were all right at horse-drawn speeds on Macadam's fairly smooth roads, but the inventors had to overtake the stage-coaches to prove their point. At 10 mph they might have kept to their schedules but too often a crazy burst at 20 or even 30 mph was followed by the disgruntled passengers walking home.

Perhaps the most successful builders of steam coaches were Walter Hancock and Goldsworthy Gurney, who both became active around 1825. The Hancock machine had a vertical engine, driving the axle through a chain, and no differential. Tyre slip was sufficient for allowing wide curves to be taken, but in order to turn sharp corners, clutches on the wheels could be unscrewed by an assistant. Gurney mounted his horizontal twin-cylinder engine on an unsprung sub-frame, the rear wheels being attached directly to the crankshaft, no doubt with improvised differential arrangements like Hancock's.

Both these designs were successful and Walter Hancock ran coach services for 16 years, though neither he nor Gurney made money from their projects. Their vehicles could not be called cars by the widest stretch of the imagination and required an engineer and fireman to operate them, but later on, Thomas Rickett made a few light 3-wheeled steam locomotives for owner-drivers, though a stoker was still carried at the rear to shovel in the coke.

G.MORTON, Del.

Published by Tho.

*The Guide or Engineer is seated in front, having a lever rod from the two guide wheels to turn & direct the Ca_ _ind part of the Coach contains, the machinery for producing the Steam, on a novel & secure principle, which is co_ _ontains about 60 Gallons of water, is placed under the body of the Coach & is its full length & breadth___the C_ _roduced will be dispelled by the action of the Vehicle ____ At different stations on a journey the Coach receives_ _ravelling is intended to be from 8 to 10 miles per hour___ The present Steam Carriage carries 6 inside & 12 outside It has been constructed by Mr Gol_*

Goldsworthy Gurney's splendid steam coach in action in
pre-breathalyser days, about 1825.

26 Haymarket. London.

PYALL. Sculp

another at his right hand connecting with the main Steam Pipe by which he regulates the motion of the Vehicle — th
by Pipes to the Cylinders beneath & by its action on the hind wheels sets the Carriage in motion — The Tank whi
are fixed on the top of the hind boot & as Coke is used for fuel, there will be no smoke while any hot or ratified a
plies of fuel & water — the full length of the Carriage is from 15 to 20 feet & its weight about 2 Tons ——— The rate
rs — the front Boot contains the Luggage ———
y Gurney the Inventor & Patentee.

The Marquis of Stafford took delivery in 1858 and the Earl of Caithness soon after him. Accounts still survive of some remarkable journeys made by the Earl in the very north of Scotland, notably his ascent of the Ord of Caithness, but though his machine was built to run at 10 mph, he claimed to have touched 19 mph. With 3 wheels and iron tyres, that must have been a terrifying experience. In France, Amédée Bollée made many steam vehicles of advanced design and remarkable performance, but again they were not really suitable for use as private cars, requiring a stoker and engineer in overalls.

In 1830 came the railway boom, when everybody went railway-mad and tried to buy shares. The great George Stephenson had said that steam engines needed smooth metal rails to run upon and certainly the problems were far less than those of travelling on ordinary roads. At first, the upper crust were catered for on the railways and gentlemen could have their own carriages, giving seclusion from the hoi-polloi, while trains stopped at private stations for stately homes.

The Duke of Sutherland had his own personal railway, which was connected up to the Highland Railway from his seat, Dunrobin Castle. He drove his own engine, a 2–4–0 tank with 4-ft coupled wheels, weighing 21 tons. When his son became Duke, he had a larger engine built, dark green with black bands and yellow lines, with a full-width leather-upholstered seat for his guests actually in the driver's cab. What fun it was to be a duke in those days!

Let us get back to the road.

The turnpike operators put up their tolls for steam coaches, to such an extent that they were virtually forced off the road. They gave as their excuse the extra wear on the road surface, but it was really to placate the owners of the stage-coaches, their best customers. Little did they realize that the railways would put an end to most of the stage-coaches and bankrupt them. Travel by rail was fast and cheap, so the turnpikes failed, the roads were again neglected, and many country hotels degenerated into mere ale-houses.

As if all that were not enough, a law was passed in Britain in 1865 to make a man walk ahead of the steam-traction engine. It was not originally meant for steam coaches, of course, but Members of Parliament, most of whom had railway shares, saw to it that these rivals to the trains were included. This stupid law killed the British steam coach, while Amédée Bollée and his friends were free to enjoy the *Routes Nationales*. It would also ensure the leadership of French and German cars when the first automobiles were being developed.

This was all very stupid, for the law itself was a good one. The first traction engines were a pretty frightening sight when they suddenly came into view on a country lane. Belching smoke and steam, they terrified animals and the people who were driving them, for countrymen had heard that steam boilers exploded without warning. As they only travelled at a slow walking pace, it was a kind thought to have a man well in front to prepare people for the arrival of the monster.

It was the bicycle craze that brought people back to the roads and made them realize how much they were missing on the railways. The high bicycle or 'ordinary' was impossible for ladies, even if they were willing to wear the new and shocking bloomers. The safety bicycle altered all that in 1885 and when the pneumatic tyre arrived in 1890, it made the 2-wheeler both fast and comfortable. Even the aristocracy 'went for a spin', and the fashionable ladies in the glossy magazines were all leaning against their cycles when they had their likeness taken.

More important, the bicycle gave individual transport. People could come and go as they wished, with no servants waiting to go home and no animals to consider. Above all, there were no railway timetables to spoil a day in the country with their tyranny.

Cycling was 'a thrill', as one swooped downhill, ridiculing the fastest coach. Freedom is man's most precious possession and the bicycle gave freedom as no other vehicle had ever done. The disadvantage was that it was very tiring and you had to be physically fit to enjoy it. The stage was set for a light form of transportation that would need no pedalling and no stoker.

A summons issued in the days when it was illegal to drive in England without a man walking in front.

In the Metropolitan Police District.

To *Walter C Bersey*
of *39 Victoria Street, Westminster*

INFORMATION has been laid
this day by *George Dixon*
for that you, on the *20th* Day of *october*
in the Year One Thousand Eight Hundred and Ninety *six*
at *a certain public highway, to wit*
Parliament Street
within the District aforesaid, *and being the owner and*
having the charge of a locomotive
propelled by other than animal power,
to wit, a motor car, did unlawfully neglect
to have such locomotive whilst in motion
preceded by at least 20 yards by a
person on foot
Contrary to the Statute etc

YOU ARE THEREFORE hereby summoned to appear before the Court of Summary Jurisdiction, sitting at the *Bow Street* Police Court on *Satur* day the *31st* day of *october*
at the hour of *two* in the *after* noon, to answer to the said *information*.

Dated the *23d* day of *october*
One Thousand Eight Hundred and Ninety *six*

H Lushington

Sch. I.—2.
SUMMONS.
GENERAL FORM SUMMARY CASES.
S. J. A. Rules, 1886—2.

One of the Magistrates of the Police Courts of the Metropolis.

W B & L (484c) — 64151—10000-6-96

2

Le Système Panhard

1890-1902

The Panhard et Levassor of 1891, with the engine moved to the front, like countless cars that were to follow. The object was to provide easy entry by a carriage step, without climbing over the muddy wheel.

Though men had travelled on the road in steam vehicles at the beginning of the nineteenth century, these heavy coaches were not the ancestors of the car. They had been superseded by the railways, which provided fast, long-distance travel such as the world had never known. Yet, by the last quarter of the century, engineers were making renewed attempts to produce a practical, mechanically propelled road vehicle.

Their machines were not originally intended to be in any way competitive with trains, nor even with the carriages, horses, and servants of the rich. The first cars were humble little vehicles, with about the accommodation and performance of a pony and trap. The pioneers were not going to make the same mistakes as the original steam-coach proprietors and they were happy to learn to walk before they could run.

Perhaps we may allow ourselves the benefit of hindsight. At the beginning of the automobile era, there was much discussion about whether the prime mover of the future would be steam, internal combustion, or electricity. We do not yet know the final outcome of that contest, of course, but for our present purpose the internal-combustion engine has won hands down. It therefore seems reasonable to investigate the beginnings of the petrol-driven car first.

The first internal-combustion engines were the gas engines, running on ordinary town-lighting gas, which were used in factories and workshops. When the compression stroke was added to the cycle of operations, the 4-stroke gas engine became more powerful and economical than any steam plant of comparable weight or size. At first, it seemed that August Otto held a patent for the so-called Otto cycle, which could cripple any would-be car makers. When it was found that Beau de Rochas had taken out an earlier patent, Otto's claim was set aside, which allowed Karl Benz, for one, to abandon his 2-stroke experiments and adapt the 4-stroke gas engine to hydrocarbon fuel in liquid form.

He did just that, and with his lightened gas engine he also took the flat belts and pulleys that then transmitted all the power used in workshops. When he drove around in Mannheim in 1885 or the beginning of 1886, he may not have been the first motorist but he was certainly the first manufacturer to offer cars for sale.

In Germany, nobody wanted a car – not that sort of car, anyway. It was not really practical and had only three wheels, because Benz could not work out the correct geometry for steering 2 stub-axles, and he feared that horse-type steering, with a centre-pivoted axle, would be hard to hold straight, by hand, over bumps. Had he known that Lenkensperger had laid down the principle of compensated steering in an ancient patent of 1818, he would have been saved some sleepless nights, but he didn't find out until 1893.

If the severely practical Germans didn't like the Benz, the French thought it was a delightful toy. The first customer was one Emile Roger, who took a Benz back to Paris and became an agent. Subsequently, the Benz was built under licence in both France and England under various names.

Any history of the automobile must start with these four. Without them, the car would presumably have been born eventually, but precious years would have been lost.

Karl Benz

Gottlieb Daimler

Emile Levassor

Louise Sarazin

The first prototype Benz had an engine developing less than 1 horsepower from its 1-litre single cylinder at 250 rpm. It had a fast and loose pulley arrangement instead of a clutch and the flat belt drove a differential, from which the power was transmitted to the rear wheels by a pair of side chains. There was no gearchange.

Obviously, such a machine was hopelessly under-powered and the first 3-wheelers supplied to the public had a larger engine developing about 1½ bhp and a low speed, achieved by interposing a chain and sprockets between the engine and the driving pulley when hills had to be climbed. The most popular Benz was the later 4-wheeler, which had engines ranging from 3 to 5½ bhp and a 2-speed 'gear' using 2 separate crossed belts. By the end of the century, an extra Crypto reduction gear could be supplied to those living in hilly regions and even a huge 2-cylinder engine, still of open-crankshaft gas-engine type, was offered. By then, however, the Benz was hopelessly out-of-date.

Such a crude vehicle had nothing to do with the upper crust, but it was sometimes bought by the wealthy as a new form of amusement, before other cars were available. It was scarcely suitable for attending social functions, however. Every 25 miles, one stopped to grease the bearings of the crankshaft, after which one pulled on the rim of the flywheel to make the engine start. Thus, a Benz driver finished any journey with grease up to the elbows and broken finger nails from shortening stretched belts. The solid rubber tyres and vertical

Benz nineteenth-century horseless carriage. The open-crankshaft engine and belt-drive by fast and loose pulleys was a hangover from Victorian workshop practice, which could never be adapted to reasonably rapid vehicles.

The mid-engined Panhard et Levassor prototype of 1890, obviously adapted from a horse-drawn vehicle. The engine was Gottlieb Daimler's all-enclosed high-speed masterpiece.

steering handle made the car a bit lively to conduct, even though its ultimate maximum was only 14 mph, while the brakes were rather gradual in action and all the controls were awkwardly placed.

To travel in, or rather on, a Benz is a curious experience, for none of the sounds or sensations can be compared with motoring as we know it. The driver does not pray for more speed, because he knows that the vehicle would become uncontrollable, but even quite moderate hills are taken at a slow walking pace, which really is a bore. Most Benz owners got rid of them as soon as something less crude was available and old Karl Benz nearly ruined his firm by making these cars for too long.

Nevertheless, the early Benz was the first working man's car. They could be picked up for a song when their original owners grew tired of them and they were very cheap to run. The heavy cost of the early pneumatic tyres was avoided and the engine ran so slowly that it never wore out. In smart society, the Benz was soon regarded as a joke in rather bad taste, but it continued to run slowly and reliably as it descended the social scale, until its engine was used to drive a sawbench or a chaff-cutter, for which the flat belt was ready-made.

It is curious that in another part of Germany, Gottlieb Daimler was developing an internal-combustion engine for automotive purposes at the same time. The wizard of Cannstatt never met Benz and his engine was designed from first principles, bearing no relationship to stationary power plants. It was planned *ab initio* for high speeds of rotation and, to ensure proper lubrication at these velocities, the crankshaft was enclosed so that the oil would not be flung away. Though the first Daimler engines only ran at 750 rpm, they had the potential for development which has resulted in the high-speed engine of today.

The first Daimler engines were single-cylinder units but a narrow-angle v-twin, with the cylinders set extremely close together, was for a long time the main product. Gottlieb Daimler did not at first propose to build cars, intending his engines to be used by other manufacturers for boats, tramways, motorcycles and any other automotive purpose. When the Benz patent specification was published early in 1886, he thought he had better build a car pretty quickly, but it was only a crude prototype to show what his engine could do. Later on, he was involved in the production himself of DMG and Cannstatt-Daimler cars, but of that more anon.

Once again, the Germans saw no future in the automobile, but Daimler sold the agency and patent rights of his engines, for France and Belgium, to Edouard Sarazin. In order to secure his rights, Sarazin had 3 engines built to Daimler's drawings in Paris and he made a choice which was to have far-reaching effects on the future of the motor car. He chose the firm of Panhard et Levassor to make his engines, because he could trust them to respect his confidences and he thought very highly of Emile Levassor.

Levassor was extremely enthusiastic about the new engine and began to get ideas about building a car to exploit it. Sarazin was delighted, but before the friends could go any further, he was taken desperately ill. On his death-bed in 1887 he told his wife that she must go ahead with this project, saying that it had '... a future one cannot even imagine!' Louise Sarazin therefore disposed of his Swedish steel interests, which would eventually have made her a very wealthy woman, and staked her future on the somewhat problematical prospects of the horseless carriage.

She wrote to Daimler, asking for her husband's rights to be transferred to her, and then travelled to Cannstatt to convince him that she was in earnest. He found her a very able business woman and agreed to go ahead, so she returned to Levassor, where a shock awaited her. The brilliant engineer was excessively timid with women and he hated doing business with them; it was only with the greatest difficulty that she eventually persuaded him to continue the work. However, he was keen to meet the great Daimler and agreed to accompany her on her next visit to Cannstatt.

Daimler and Levassor immediately became firm friends and on the return journey the cold Levassor thawed out sufficiently to become engaged to the young widow – they were married in 1890. Miraculously, all the correspondence from those momentous days has survived and some long extracts are reproduced in that excellent book by Jacques Ickx, *Ainsi Naquit l'Automobile* – it is interesting that Daimler wrote excellent French in a clear hand.

In the contract, Levassor agreed to pay a 12 per cent royalty on 30 engines a year, but, being a pessimist, he doubted whether he could sell so many cars. Accordingly, he approached Armand Peugeot, the bicycle manufacturer, to see if he would take some of them. Peugeot was having a terrible time trying to develop a car powered by a Serpollet steam engine, and he jumped at the chance. Thus was born the French motor industry, which was to lead the world.

Armand Peugeot's designer, Rigoulot, thought it logical to mount the engine near the back wheels that it was to drive and he produced a neat little tubular chassis, which was easy for a cycle manufacturer to make. Levassor first put the engine in the middle of the car, with the 4 occupants back to back and the compact power plant between them. However, Daimler's little v-twin was not really powerful enough for a 4-seater built on Levassor's principle, *'faites lourd, vous ferez solide!'* The next Panhard et Levassor survives in the museum at Compiègne and has the engine ahead of the rear wheels of a 2-seater, which it drives by side chains. Four of these were sold to customers in 1891 – copies of the invoices still exist – and then something extraordinary happened.

Levassor put the engine at the front, thus setting a fashion that virtually every manufacturer would follow for the next 40 years. It drove through a clutch, brush-type at first and then a cone, and a 3-speed gearbox which was all gears and no box – the gears ran in the open air, lubricated with thick grease – and road dust! At the rear of the gearbox was a bevel gear, with a sprocket that was connected by a single chain to the rear axle. Why Levassor temporarily foresook side chains for a single central chain, nobody knows.

It is also quite weird that he did not use the orthodox differential, though it had been applied to a steam wagon by Pecqueur in 1828 and to a tricycle by Roberts in 1831. It is just as incomprehensible now as the initial failure of Benz to work out the steering geometry of 2 front wheels. Yet, Levassor used a crude friction-type 'false differential' and he did not revert to side chains and a bevel-gear differential until 1895, though Rigoulot had used them on all his Peugeots.

When Levassor put the engine at the front of the car, he ensured that the Panhard would win all the forthcoming motor races and would also be the preferred carriage of the upper crust. The forward mounting permitted the engine to expand, which it did at a fantastic rate in the first few motoring years. By endeavouring to keep all the machinery further back the other manufacturers, particularly Peugeot, would find it almost impossible later on to accommodate the big, 4-cylinder engines, which were at first very long.

Levassor personally wanted his cars to look as much like the current horse-drawn vehicles as possible, so he made the engine bonnet as small as he could, disguising it as a luggage locker. He was not to know that his upper-crust clients would regard the bonnet as a status symbol, the longer the better to denote a powerful engine. Indeed, those who were still trying to sell cars with engines located elsewhere were later forced to place dummy bonnets at the front of their chassis.

It has been suggested that Levassor showed amazing foresight in adopting a *système* which would eventually allow much larger engines to be used to advantage, at a time when only the tiny Daimler engines of 3 hp (1,058 cc) or 3½ hp (1,235 cc) existed. The answer is that the change in design was entirely fortuitous. With the engine behind, the driver and passenger had to climb over the muddy front wheels, as in a horse-drawn 4-wheeler. The voluminous skirts worn by ladies were inevitably soiled by this acrobatic feat and so Levassor moved the seat back behind the front wheels and put the engine between them; to a newly and very happily married man, such considerations were of more importance than mere mechanical convenience. Instead of the *Système Panhard*, perhaps it should have been called the *Système Louise Levassor*!

In 1892, Levassor wrote to Daimler saying that he had put 'bandages of rubber' round the wheels which made the car 'almost silent'. In 1895, he produced an improved model with a bevel differential, side chains, and a new engine which Daimler and Wilhelm Maybach had designed. This was called the *Phénix* and had the 2 cylinders in line, with dimensions of 80 × 120 mm (1,206 cc), conservatively rated at 4 hp.

It was with such a car that Levassor won the first great motor race, Paris–Bordeaux–Paris. He drove up to the starting line with Louise beside him, but she stepped down in favour of a professional *mécanicien* called D'Hostingue for the race, who very properly wore a bowler hat. Two days and 2 nights later, this incredible pair returned to Paris, the 53-year-old Levassor having driven all the way, with oil and candle lights at night to cast a feeble glimmer on the white dust of the macadam. They travelled for 48 hours and 48 minutes, without a single stop for rest, to average 15 mph for 732 miles. *Formidable!* At the finishing line, they were welcomed by Louise and old Gottlieb Daimler, the former in tears and the latter dancing, as well he might with his engines driving the first four cars, a mixed bag of Panhards and Peugeots. The Benz, with its single-cylinder gas engine stretched to 3-litre capacity, was outclassed, finishing 16 hours later, while the powerful steam cars had fallen by the wayside.

Thereafter, the pattern was set for the next decade, and to make the upper crust a car had to do well in the glamorous town-to-town races. As Panhards had a monopoly of racing successes for the first few years, this was *the* make to buy if you wanted the best. It is sad to relate that Emile Levassor overturned his car in the Paris–Marseille race, probably due to the direct tiller steering, which could be snatched out of the driver's hand by a hole in the road. He never fully recovered and was struck down at his drawing board while inventing a new, electrically operated clutch, less than 2 years after his great victory. His Paris–Bordeaux–Paris triumph is commemorated by a monument, which still stands at the Porte Maillot in Paris.

After Levassor's death, the Panhard racing team was led by one of the firm's directors, an aristocrat with tremendous panache, the

Paris–Bordeaux–Paris 1895. Emile Levassor, with his mechanic D'Hostingue beside him, after completing the course in 48 hours and 48 minutes without a single stop for rest.

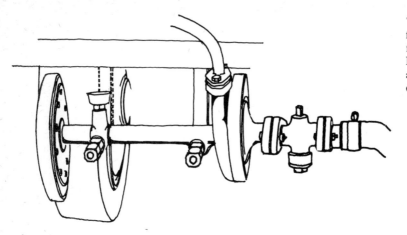

bearded Chevalier René de Knyff. My old friend Mike Sassoon – who was probably the only octogenarian to fly his own aeroplane – told me a typical de Knyff story. Mike had gone to Paris for the motor show and was lucky enough to see the Chevalier arrive. The great racing Panhard thundered into view over the wet cobbles when, with a jab on the brakes and a flick of the steering, the driver skidded it through 180 degrees and rolled neatly backwards into his reserved *parking*, leaving his man Aristide to keep the crowd from fingering the shimmering brasswork.

The racing Panhards were of identical design to the standard touring cars, except that the engines rapidly increased in size. These engines were at first of Daimler's Phénix type, later replaced by Panhard's own Centaure, which differed in having the head cast integrally with the cylinders. In both cases, the crank-case was an aluminium casting, superb even by the standards of today, and the cast-iron cylinders were in pairs.

All Panhards had side exhaust valves with overhead, suction-operated automatic inlet valves and were cooled by water carried in a large copper tank under the car, with forced circulation from a centrifugal pump, driven at high speed by friction from the big flywheel. As the engines grew larger, a gilled tube radiator was added, at first under the rear part of the car but later at the front of the bonnet ahead of the engine, thus starting a new fashion which persists to this day.

Ignition was by Daimler's red-hot platinum tube and burner, only superseded by battery-operated trembler coils and a com-mutator in 1900, though the burners were still carried for emergencies, both on the racing cars and the standard productions, for a number of years. The dangerous direct steering by *queue de vache* was at last replaced by a wheel and reduction gear about 1898. By then the transmission gears had long retreated into an aluminium box, instead of toiling in the open air, and pneumatic tyres had been adopted.

In 1897, the 2-cylinder 90 × 130 mm engine had a capacity of 1,654 cc, a 3·3-litre 4-cylinder with the same bore and stroke becoming available in 1899. The 2-cylinder version was to become

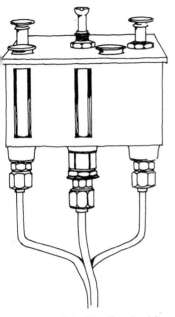

Panhard double oil tank with adjustable drip feed in centre and hand pumps at each end, also two glass oil level gauges and central glass for counting drips per minute.

Panhard's popular model, one of which I have been driving in veteran car events for many years; though this is by no means an upper-crust car, it is identical in all but its body to the earlier works racers. The quality Panhard was the 4-cylinder, which was also made in rapidly increasing sizes for racing at 4·4, 5·3, and 7·4 litres. Though the 3·3-litre engine normally sufficed for touring, wealthy clients were allowed to specify the larger power units.

A special racing engine was built by Panhard et Levassor in 1902. To save weight, it had separate cylinders, with corrugated copper water jackets soldered in place, and it was the first of the giants which made racing so exciting – and dangerous. The 13-litre engine was rated at 70 hp, though it developed about 90 bhp, and the chassis was of standard Panhard design, except for a transverse front spring instead of semi-elliptics, which was also used on the 1902 version of the 40 hp racer.

Right from the beginning, all Panhards had wooden chassis frames reinforced with steel at points of stress. There were curious variations in suspension, the 1891–4 model having semi-elliptic springs behind and full-elliptics in front, while the 1895 car had full-elliptics all round, and the 1897–9 type full-elliptics behind and semi-elliptics in front, with only semi-elliptics thereafter on the production cars. Obviously the bumpy French roads were setting suspension problems as speed increased; it had risen from 14 mph in 1891 to 80 mph by the 70 hp Panhard in 1902, though few cars exceeded 30 mph on the public roads and even this speed was illegal in England.

The Panhards of this period all had constant-speed engines with centrifugal governors, which allowed them to run at about 800 rpm normally. A pedal, with a small hand-lever attached to it, could be pressed down to risk a short burst of revs above the governed speed, or lifted by hand to slow the engine a little and avoid 'racing' when idling in neutral; nevertheless, an engine with automatic inlet valves and tube ignition was incapable of wide speed variations. To accommodate the governed engine, the hand and foot brakes were both coupled to the clutch, which was held out while the car was being slowed; therefore the engine could not be used to assist braking.

Though the technique is entirely different, an early Panhard is delightful to drive. The steering is extremely quick and the narrow tyres give a good feel of the road. It is pleasant to let the governed engine choose its own speed, shutting off downhill and calling on all the horses for a slight up-grade. To change down, one lets the car 'pull against the collar' on a hill, then double-declutches while moving the lever, the governor revving up the engine in neutral and ensuring a perfectly silent engagement of the gears. Up-changes are slow but easily judged, with the clutch pedal held right down. The brakes are adequate but considerable care must be exercised on steep descents. A long day's drive on secondary roads can be rather tiring, largely due to the galloping movement of the short-wheelbase chassis on its soft, undamped springs, but this is a real car and not a mere horseless carriage like the Benz.

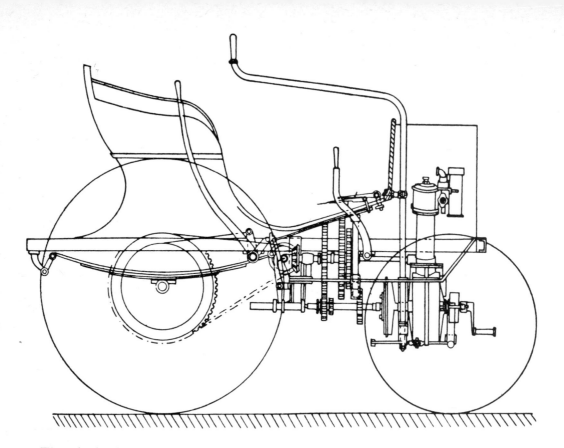

Though the first Panhards were 2-seaters, a 4-seater tonneau with a central rear door was soon the most popular body style. A long chassis was available to carry bodies with extra seating capacity and some very lofty closed coachwork was occasionally fitted on cars intended for town work, though it adversely affected performance and handling.

Of the rivals of the great *marque*, Mors changed over from a rear engine to the *Système Panhard* and started to win races, while even Peugeot tired of their huge, rear-mounted 2-cylinder engine and followed the crowd; the De Dietrich actually looked like a Panhard.

The Marquis de Dion lost patience with his heavy racing steam cars and went to the other extreme, selling tricycles and small cars powered with high-speed single-cylinder engines, which were soon moved from the rear to the Panhard position; transmission was, of course, by the famous De Dion axle instead of by chains. Not an upper-crust car, the De Dion Bouton was nevertheless regarded as *chic* for ladies to use in Paris; besides, a car made by a marquis can't be bad, can it?

The most important newcomer, among a host of French cars which are now forgotten, was Louis Renault, who had learnt engineering in the steam-locomotive workshops of Delaunay-Belleville. Renault started making cars in 1898 and he took the *Système Panhard* a stage further, his machine having not only the first gearbox giving a direct drive in top gear, but also the first example of a universally jointed propeller shaft with a fully sprung live rear axle.

Le Système Panhard. With the engine in front, driving by clutch and gearbox to the rear wheels, it set a fashion in 1891 that virtually every manufacturer followed eventually.

34

Baron de Crawhez driving the 70 hp 13-litre Panhard et Levassor in Paris–Madrid, 'the race to death', which was stopped at Bordeaux.

Racing and commercial success were synonymous and Renault made the small-car classes their own, moving on to big-car racing, and victory in the first Grand Prix, in due course.

The Renault had the great advantage of shaft drive, with no filthy chains just where the coachbuilder wanted to put the rear doors of his limousine. It was commonly thought that shaft drive was unsuitable for very powerful cars, but the Renault was the town car *par excellence*, its chassis being ideal for the mounting of closed coachwork. The Renault was patronized by royalty, but the name was perhaps a little tarnished by the appearance of taxicabs with the well-known coalscuttle bonnet on the streets of Paris and London.

The French motor industry was by far the biggest in the world and a man wanting a high-quality car would buy a French make as a matter of course. Motor racing was invented by the French and their works teams had a virtual monopoly of victories until the Mercédès era. Whether the Panhard, the Mors, the De Dietrich, or the Brasier was the best of the upper-crust cars is a matter of opinion, but before 1903 there is no doubt that a French car built on the *Système Panhard* was the best in the world.

In England, motoring was virtually illegal before 1896, though a few brave pioneers ran the gauntlet of police persecution. Traditionally, the British ruling classes worshipped the horse and they did not take kindly to the new locomotion. There were many people who secretly longed for a car but dared not risk the disapproval of their servants.

It is not realized nowadays how completely many families were dominated by those whom they nominally employed. Every social function was at risk because the dreaded message could come from the stables that the horses were lame or had gone down with one of the many ailments to which they were heir. If the coachman didn't want to turn out, he could always give the horses dusty hay to make them cough, or use some other tricks which are best not mentioned here.

A.B. Filson Young, in his charming book, *The Complete Motorist*, advocated the purchase of a small utility car, such as a wagonette or station bus, as a means of breaking the ice with the stable staff.

Some people, I know, are too much afraid of their coachmen and head grooms to suggest the keeping of the motor-car after which in their hearts they hanker; but if they will try this plan as a beginning, treating the motor-car not as a serious or important vehicle in itself, but merely as a dishonoured drudge, retained to wait upon and relieve the delicate inmates of the stable, they will find opinion in the harness-room rapidly veering round in favour of the new-fangled machines.

The car brought its own problems to the stately homes of England, for if you had a Panhard or a Mors it was only natural to engage a French chauffeur or mechanic, who was apt to cause a considerable upset below stairs. French chauffeurs proved even more difficult to handle than British coachmen, and most of them were too elegant to wash or grease a car – they demanded an under-

The Hon Charles Rolls, with the Duchess of York, later Queen Mary, in a 4-cylinder Panhard et Levassor with pneumatic tyres, outside his ancestral home.

mechanic for that. Many British chauffeurs were excellent, with a real pride in their smooth driving, and upper-crust employers would soon prefer them, both in the USA and on the Continent as well as in Great Britain.

British cars made a late start and their time was yet to come, though the Lanchester was a brilliant design which was unfortunately a bit too clever for the average garage man. However, the Lanchester had the tremendous advantage of a foolproof gear-change and its suspension was very comfortable on indifferent country roads. The first Coventry Daimlers were built under licence from Cannstatt and were rather heavy and slow, but after a complete reorganization the company was to produce some notable high-performance cars before long.

As to the alternative modes of propulsion, the steam car was never really popular in Europe, though De Dion Bouton and Bollée showed great speed at the very beginning of racing. These were heavy locomotives, however, demanding a black-faced crew to run them. Alfred C. Harmsworth had a Serpollet, with a luxurious closed body by the great coachbuilder Kellner, of which he wrote enthusiastically in the Badminton Library book, *Motors*. As he carried two servants to run the car on his Continental tours, it can be assumed that it was not a proposition for an owner-driver. Serpollet cars proved very reliable in long-distance races but they were out-classed as petrol cars grew faster.

There are those of us who will always have a sentimental attach-ment for the steam engine and in theory a steam luxury car should be silent and infinitely flexible, with no gearchanging. In practice, how-ever, a simple steam car needs a lot of skill to drive in traffic and once you start adding automatic devices to overcome this, the steamer becomes far more complicated than the internal-combustion vehicle. In fact, steam cars died because they used about twice as much fuel as comparable internal-combustion cars, and even the very wealthy dislike wasting money, with nothing to show for it.

As for electric cars, the electric brougham was an enormous suc-cess in the first few years of the century. In Paris, and especially in London, every lady of fashion had one. They were silent, vibration-less, and did not stink – nobody called it pollution then – and they were smart-looking little vehicles. At first, the driver perched behind at a great height, exactly as in a hansom cab, but later the chauffeur and footman sat in front, thus blocking the view of the occupants. The last broughams had very low seats for the men out-side and the interior seat was raised, so that milady and friend could see and be seen.

The electric brougham was the perfect upper-crust town car, it would seem. Unfortunately, few town houses possessed charging facilities and even when they did, chauffeurs could never understand the maintenance of the accumulators, which resulted in embarras-sing breakdowns with no power and no lights. As a result, most of the broughams were later owned and maintained by companies which hired them out, with their own trained drivers, on a yearly basis. These men had the sense to nip into one of the firm's depots for a quick charge whenever they could and the service they gave was excellent.

It is sad that the electric-brougham firms simply folded up because the cost of re-plating the batteries was enormous. The life of a battery in London traffic might be only a few weeks, for the con-tinuous rapid charging and discharging played havoc with them. Apart from the batteries, these little carriages were totally without faults, which means that the electric town car will immediately return, if and when a light accumulator with a long life is invented.

Curiously enough, petrol cars came a poor third numerically in the USA, steam and electric vehicles being much more popular. The reason was that the American steam and electric cars were little buggies of the lightest construction, which were only used around the towns and cities. Most of the small American steam cars were of the simplest possible design and though they seemed little more than toys, they could give reasonable service to a sympathetic owner who did not ask too much of them. The electrics, because they were clean and always ready to start, were favoured by professional men, such as doctors, in spite of their very limited range between charges.

For serious motoring in the USA, however, a very tough type of car was needed. Distances were vast and many of the roads were almost impassable unless one had a fairly light car with great pulling power. Pictures of early motoring conditions in the USA show why many European cars were altogether too delicate to withstand such a hammering. If a car could struggle, day after day, up to its axles in mud, it was good enough, while coach paint and varnish were superfluous. Many early American cars looked a bit rough in a showroom, but for functional transportation they were incomparable and they have always had my warmest admiration. To say that they were not upper-crust material is not to belittle them in any way.

The period covered by this chapter starts at the very beginning of motoring. The pioneers tackled an infinitely greater task than the railway engineers had had to face. To make a machine that will run on a flat track is one thing but to construct a vehicle that will cope with the steep hills, the sharp corners, the bumps, and the unexpected emergencies of the road is quite another. Railway locomotives might not have been so reliable if they had been sprayed every day with dust or mud and they would certainly not have withstood being handled by clumsy amateur drivers and mechanics.

Knowing that all these obstacles were in their path, the devoted engineers pressed on. In fact, within a very short time after the first feeble chuff-chuff-chuff was heard, their first cars became quite effective little vehicles. That the motor-car advanced beyond the pony and trap stage is entirely due to the pneumatic tyre. At first, it seemed impossible to carry a car on bladders of air, which had to roll over sharp stones and flints while constantly subjected to the abrasion of grit and the percussion of potholes.

If you had watched those very first motor races, you would have seen 2 brothers, Edouard and André Michelin, driving a racing car with wheels that looked curiously fat compared with the solid rubber tyres used by the other competitors. When they were going, nobody could touch them, but each short speed burst was followed by a terrible bang or a heartbreaking hiss of escaping air. Then it was slaving at tyre levers and pumps, while the others disappeared in the distance.

Poor Edouard and André never won a race, but by risking their new product in the public gaze, and doing all the hard work with their own hands, they learnt incredibly quickly. In 2 years, all racing cars were on pneumatic tyres and fast touring cars soon followed them. An expensive luxury at first, they became an indispensable part of every car. Perhaps sometimes, when we are roaring down the motorway at high speed without giving a thought to our tyres, we should remember the Michelin brothers, hundreds of miles behind Emile Levassor, changing yet another tyre with bleeding hands, on that interminable road from Paris to Bordeaux and back again in 1895. There is a picture of them, toiling in this first great race, among those beautifully painted tiles that adorn the Michelin building in Fulham Road, London.

3
Mercédès 1903-1906

The Victorian motor vehicle was still a horseless carriage; if it went at all it was a success and neither the manner nor the speed of its going were of great importance. In the first years of the new century, the progress in design was fantastic. Cars were improved in every way but the great obsession was speed.

Even in England, where the roads were most unsuitable, there was an insistent demand among the rich for ever more powerful cars. In France, where the long, straight roads encouraged this mania, it was considered rather amusing to drive with a total lack of consideration for slower traffic. Some of the advertisements for French cars of the period are almost incredible now. They depict the vehicle travelling at supersonic speed in a cloud of dust, while pedestrians and horses collapse in terror in the ditch and chickens try vainly to escape, with feathers everywhere.

Cars were becoming faster, larger and heavier, which emphasized the greatest disadvantage of the water-bound macadam road. In dry weather, the top coating became a thick layer of dust. The suction caused by the passage of a fast car lifted the dust to a great height behind it, the swirling, opaque cloud remaining suspended in the air for some time afterwards. When it descended, it spread outwards and adhered in a filthy layer to roadside gardens and crops.

The disturbed airflow behind an open touring car could cause the dust to invade the rear seats and almost suffocate the unfortunate passengers. This was avoided by building the back panel of the body very high and also by allowing the folded hood to project a long way behind, sloped at an angle of 45 degrees or so, to hold the dust down. This was rather a blow-you-Jack philosophy, of course, and nothing was done to keep the grime off the other unfortunate road users. Nevertheless, some of these great, high-backed touring cars were exceedingly handsome.

It was the dust menace, far more than the craze for speed, which made motorists so unpopular in the early years of the century. Indeed, if the treatment of roads with tar or asphalt had not been evolved, the car would have had an uphill fight to survive. In the country, they were usually called 'those horrid motors' and at many a stately home the guests were bidden to arrive in proper horse-drawn carriages or not at all. It was the splendid motoring King of England who put a stop to that nonsense, for once he had swept up the drive in the royal Daimler, it was scarcely possible to prevent his subjects from defiling the gravel with similar, if slightly less distinguished, conveyances.

Police and magistrates were anti-motorists to a man and perjured evidence was accepted as a matter of course. Luckily, some country coppers were not averse to taking a bribe, if offered in a gentlemanly manner. The correct method was to fold a treasury note in the licence when it was presented for inspection and the constable could please himself, depending on the state of his thirst at the time. In their unpopularity, motorists of every class became brothers and it would be unthinkable to drive past a broken-down car without stopping to offer help. This marvellous freemasonry of the road

In France, it was considered amusing to drive so fast that all other road users were scared out of their wits.

PREVIOUS PAGES Pride of ownership – but only a very experienced driver could extend the 9-litre Mercédès to its limit and live to tell the tale, on the narrow macadam roads of 1903.

added enormously to the pleasure of motoring and is in sad contrast to the enmity which exists between most road-users today.

If dust was a serious nuisance to every user of the highway, it was a killer of racing drivers and their riding mechanics. The sheer courage involved in overtaking another car was immense and the risks were appalling. Imagine dashing into a moving cloud, with no idea how far ahead the other car was, and steering by looking upwards at the tops of the trees! This is rightly called the heroic period of motor racing, both for the daring of the drivers and for the glamour of the many-litred monsters which they sought to control.

It is scarcely surprising, in such a speed-conscious age, that the car desired above all others had many of the characteristics of the giant racers, but it was a gentle giant. If you were to ask all the present-day motoring historians which was *the* car of 1903, they would vote unanimously for the 60 hp Mercédès. Even at about £2500 – an enormous sum in those days – there was a queue to buy it which included royalty. At no time, before or since, has there been a make

Two illustrations of the anti-motoring sentiment of the early 1900s. In England, the upper crust adored the horse and detested 'those horrid motors'. It was principally the dust clouds which they left behind them that made motorists so unpopular.

which, without any question, was quite simply incomparable. There were few cars indeed, in any country, which did not show some Mercédès influence during the next few years.

The Mercédès story has been told so often that perhaps it is permissible to be brief. The Daimler Motoren Gesellschaft was producing cars at the turn of the century which had powerful engines but high and ungainly chassis, with rather indifferent

Road conditions that faced the early motorist, which made fast driving perilous and high average speeds impossible.

OVERLEAF A typical roadside scene in the early years of the century when chipped flints from the road metal could be razor-sharp and penetrated pneumatic tyres all too often.

handling qualities. By an arrangement which seems most odd nowadays, the wealthy Consul representing the Austro-Hungarian Empire in Nice, Emil Jellinek, also sold Cannstatt-Daimler cars to his aristocratic acquaintances.

He asked the firm to design a new line of cars for him, with much lower chassis and a definite high-performance image. Owing to the sales resistance of certain markets to anything with a Teutonic name, he called the new cars Mercédès, after his little daughter. In this he was wise, for one can scarcely imagine a British customer, for example, announcing proudly that he had bought a new Jellinek.

The car was the work of Paul Daimler and Wilhelm Maybach and the original 35 hp model caused a furore in 1901, as did the 40 hp of 6,785 cc in 1902. By 1903, the immortal 'Sixty' of 9,236 cc was in production, following the design of the 40 hp but having enough power to compete against specially built racing cars in international events. This was just as well, for the whole Mercédès team of 90 hp (12,711 cc) racing cars was destroyed in a factory fire, shortly before the great Gordon Bennett race of 1903. Three Sixties were borrowed back from sporting owners, stripped of their touring coachwork and fitted with hastily improvised racing 2-seaters.

It is history that a Sixty prevailed in the hands of Camille Jenatzy and that the big machines covered themselves with glory in other races and hillclimbs. It was not so much that the Mercédès contained a great many engineering novelties, for a number of its advanced features had already been seen on the same firm's Cannstatt-Daimlers. The difference was that in the Mercédès all this brilliant engineering was packaged so attractively.

The Sixty looked well enough in racing trim but it was as a luxurious open touring car that it showed its full breathtaking beauty. Because it had exposed chains driving the rear wheels, this chassis was usually fitted with the tonneau type of body, with a door in the centre of the rear panel and a carriage step, instead of side doors. This presented difficulties when a hood was fitted, however, and by far the best solution was the *Roi des Belges* type of body.

Mercédès Jellinek. The car which was named after her in 1901 replaced the Panhard as the leader of automobile fashion.

Camille Jenatzy, who won the 1903 Gordon-Bennett race in a 60 hp Mercédès, here seen in the less successful 90 hp model.

His Majesty of the Belgians preferred his cars' coachwork to be very curvaceous, rather like a Gaiety girl, and with a generous area of copiously buttoned leather upholstery; access to the rear compartment was often gained by swinging outwards half the front passenger's seat. That superb honeycomb radiator, set well back over the front axle, made the gilled tube radiators of earlier cars look crude and archaic and was soon widely copied.

Two great acetylene gas headlamps added to the impressive frontal appearance and they were as powerful as any modern quartz iodine or halogen projectors, but there was no way of reducing their dazzle. The front mudguards were flared at a rakish angle and those at the rear caught both the grease from the chains and a little of the mud from the tyres. As they usually swept upwards instead of downwards at their trailing ends, the backs of the tyres were exposed and mud was flung to a great height. Nobody was going to try to

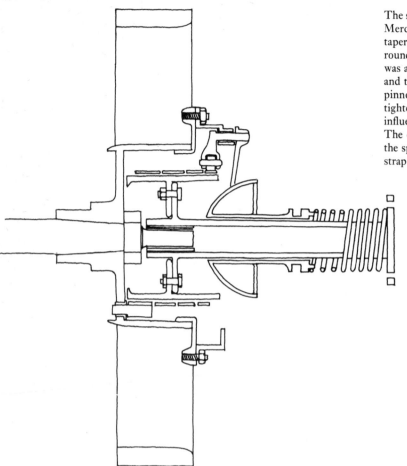

The scroll clutch of the 60 hp Mercédès was basically a tapered metal strap wound round a drum. The broad end was attached to the flywheel and the narrow end was pinned to a lever that tightened it under the influence of a strong spring. The clutch pedal compressed the spring and allowed the strap to release the drum.

follow a Sixty and so this rather anti-social characteristic was of little consequence.

Mechanically, the Mercédès followed the *Système Panhard* as far as the location of the main components was concerned. The engine was in front, just behind the radiator, and the separate gearbox was in the centre of the chassis. The huge flywheel had its spokes at an angle to form the blades of an efficient fan and an undershield fitted closely round it, stretching forward beneath the engine to the bottom of the radiator. With the bonnet closed, this meant that all the air drawn backwards by the flywheel fan must pass through the radiator honeycomb.

Instead of the big, leather-lined cone clutch of the Panhard, the Mercédès had a scroll-type clutch. This consisted of a metal strip, shaped rather like a coil spring, which wrapped round a drum. The drum was of small diameter and had considerably less inertia than the big Panhard cone, though the latter was beautifully cast in aluminium. On the other hand, the scroll clutch owed its tremendous grip to its self-wrapping servo action, which tended to make it fierce in operation, not to mention the unwrapping effect that caused tow- or push-starting to be difficult on occasion. Though the clutch of the Mercédès was sometimes criticized, there is no doubt that its small diameter and light weight were partly responsible for the incredibly easy gearchange.

The gearbox contained the bevel drive and differential, as did that of the Panhard. Where it differed completely was in the method of gear selection, for while the Panhard had 1 selector the Mercédès boasted 3. This meant that with a single selector, the gearlever had to operate in 1 plane; reverse was at the back, then neutral, followed by the 4 speeds in progression as the lever moved forward. The Mercédès gearlever worked in a gate and could be moved laterally in the central (neutral) position to pick up either of the forward gear selectors or, after releasing a safety catch, it could control the selector commanding the reverse pinion. There was a simple interlocking arrangement to prevent the simultaneous and disastrous engagement of 2 ratios.

The gate gearchange was simpler to use than the quadrant, with which it was all too easy to miss a gear by misjudging the length of movement required, and it abolished the necessity to 'come down through the box'; instead, one could move straight into neutral from top when stopping the car. Thus, although the transmission was still by side chains to the rear wheels, there were very important differences.

An even greater change was in the chassis frame itself, for whereas the *Système Panhard* embraced a wooden construction, with metal reinforcement on the corners and at points of stress, the Mercédès had an all-steel chassis. The side-members were of channel section, with cross-members riveted in place, while the engine and gearbox were bolted solidly to the frame, conferring great rigidity to the structure. The wooden chassis of French cars were remarkably light and strong, but it was usual to mount the engine and gearbox on a separate sub-frame, which left a large part of the main frame without any effective bracing.

This stiff chassis was carried on 4 long, semi-elliptic springs, almost flat in the modern manner instead of the considerable camber that was then fashionable. Light, forged steel axles were used front and rear, the steering being of worm- and nut-type with quite a rake on the column, to bring the big wheel towards the lap of the driver as he sat in his commanding position, supremely comfortable in the high bucket seat. The rear axle was a similar beam, located at the correct distance from the driving sprockets to keep the chain tension constant, by radius arms with provision for adjustment. Chain drive was considered more reliable than a live axle for very powerful cars and in any case the roadholding was much better, due to reduced unsprung weight and isolation of driveshaft torque.

Last but not least comes the great engine. This was a 9-litre 4-cylinder with dimensions of 140 mm × 150 mm (9,236 cc), the cylinders being cast in pairs and mounted on an aluminium crankcase. The exhaust valves were placed alongside the cylinders on the left side of the engine, operated from a side camshaft driven by exposed spur gears. Th same camshaft commanded overhead inlet valves through pushrods and rockers, each inlet valve having 3 concentric seats which closed 2 large annular ports in the fixed cylinder heads.

Where the Mercédès engine broke new ground was that it was a flexible unit with a fair speed range. Earlier engines nearly all had automatic, suction-operated inlet valves, which did not work satisfactorily if the air-fuel mixture were throttled to give a slow idling speed. At first the speed of the Mercédès engine was controlled by gradually reducing the lift of the mechanically operated inlet valves.

This cunning trick was performed by a toothed rack, running the length of the engine and engaging little spur wheels on the pushrods. The pushrods fitted into threaded sockets at their top ends and were simply lengthened and shortened by being screwed up and down, thus changing from full lift to practically no lift at all. It worked, too, but it was subsequently found that a butterfly in the updraught carburettor, just above the choke, gave identical results with infinitely less complication; it would appear that all the cars were converted to plain throttle control subsequently, with a hand lever on the steering wheel, though a foot accelerator was often added.

The ignition was by low-tension magneto and contact-breakers inside the cylinders. The magneto was of extremely simple construction, with a bipolar armature and a single winding of quite stout wire. Driven by exposed spur gears at crankshaft speed, it generated about 10 volts AC with 2 points of maximum flux per revolution. The spring-loaded contact breakers were necessary because the low-tension current would not jump the gap of a sparking plug. They were operated from a second camshaft on the right side of the engine, driven by yet more exposed gears.

The live points in each cylinder were mounted in soapstone insulators and connected in parallel to the magneto terminal.

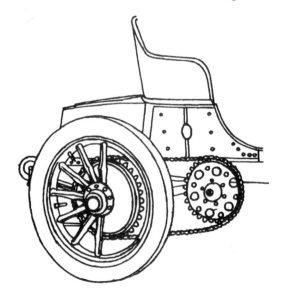

Chain drive, originally used on nearly all cars, continued to be employed for very powerful cars until the end of the Edwardian era, notably by Mercédès.

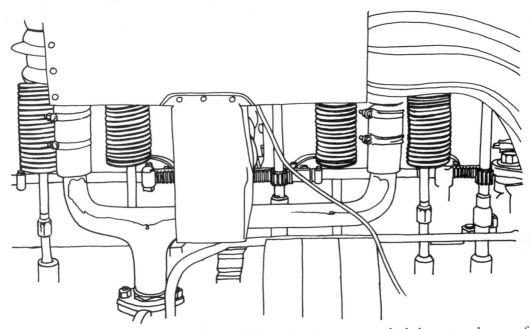

The rack and pinion arrangement for varying the lift of the overhead inlet valves of the 1903 60 hp Mercédès, later replaced by orthodox throttle control.

Through very light rods, the cams tweaked the external arms of each contact breaker in turn, causing the internal contact to 'short' the insulated one to earth and then, on suddenly being released, to open the circuit extremely rapidly by the force of the spring, thus producing a spark. In the 2 revolutions that a 4-cylinder 4-stroke engine makes in firing all its cylinders, there are 4 points of maximum flux, which are timed to coincide with the making and breaking of the contacts inside the cylinders.

The engine of the 60 hp Mercédès, showing the low-tension igniters, the throttle which replaced the variable lift inlet valves, and the numerous oil pipes from the drip-feeds on the dashboard.

Few people now understand how low-tension ignition worked, but it had many advantages. The magneto was so simple and robust that it never went wrong and the points, by their striking together, cleaned each other of any soot or carbon. For the Mercédès, which developed its 60 bhp at 1,200 rpm, it was ideal, but it was unsuitable for small, high-speed engines. There was provision in the cylinder castings for fitting additional sparking plugs if dual ignition was desired.

Lubrication was by a vast array of drip feeds on the dashboard, connected by copper pipes to all the bearings of the engine and gearbox. The drip feeds were adjusted individually to give the correct number of drops per minute, but as the oiling was on the total-loss system, and effective oil seals had not then been invented, any excess of lubrication merely came out through the bearings and fell on the road, which helped to lay the dust. A hand pump to top up the base chamber and a grease gun to lubricate the water pump were also dashboard mounted, the total oil consumption of a big Mercédès being almost as great as the petrol consumption of a modern small car.

The foot brakes operated in 2 drums on the gearbox, driven from the differential and the layshaft respectively, with provision for water cooling on long descents; the 2 pedals were side by side and sometimes a single pedal worked both brakes. A long hand-brake lever, always called the 'side-brake' at this epoch, was located beside the right-hand gearlever and retarded drums which formed part of the rear wheel sprockets. Neither the wooden wheels nor the shrunk-on steel rims were detachable, the narrow, high-pressure,

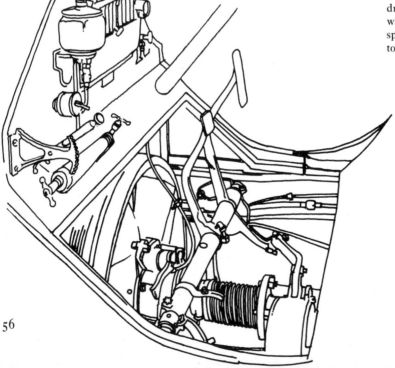

The elaborate lubrication arrangements of the 60 hp Mercédès, including multiple drip feeds, hand pump, and water pump greaser. Note the spokes of the flywheel, twisted to form a large fan.

beaded-edge tyres being levered into place with great strength and skill, as was then normal.

The Mercédès made all existing cars look out of date and though the French firms, particularly Panhard and De Dietrich, tried to carry on as though nothing had happened, the public demanded honeycomb radiators, gate gearchanges, steel chassis, and mechanically operated inlet valves. It was 'back to the drawing board' with a vengeance and firms like Fiat, which had been making pseudo-Panhards, changed over to making pseudo-Mercédès as quickly as possible. Only rugged individualists like Renault and Lanchester were able to go on making cars of their own special shapes – for some reason, the public would still buy Renaults with quadrant gear-changes when this feature was years out of date.

The 60 hp Mercédès was an incomparable touring car with only one real failing – it was remarkably difficult to start from cold. There was a half-compression device, operated by a handle beneath the radiator, which slid the camshaft along to engage extra exhaust cams. In spite of this, it took very great strength to crank a 9-litre engine full of cold, sticky oil – and 1903 oil was extremely thick. No doubt most owners had a full-time chauffeur or mechanic on the premises who was responsible for getting the engine going in the morning, but reasonably fast cranking was necessary to coax a spark from the magneto.

To appreciate how immense the performance of the Sixty was, it is necessary to recall how slowly other cars went in 1903. A typical small car would have a maximum speed no higher than 30 mph and would climb a 1-in-10 gradient at 5 to 7 mph in bottom gear, steeper hills than 1-in-8 requiring the passengers to dismount. A proud automobilist would claim that he had surmounted Westerham Hill 'without shedding'. A medium-sized 4-cylinder car would attain 40 to 45 mph and 'romp up Westerham with power in hand, old man'.

The 60 hp Mercédès, when stripped for racing, would attain 80 mph and hold it for as long as the road permitted. With a large open touring body, mudguards, and lamps, a maximum around 65 mph would be realistic. It took hills at a higher speed than many other cars of its time would reach on the level and with none of the gear noise and vibrations of lesser breeds.

Having driven the Sixty, I am almost at a loss to put the experience into words. As the engine idles, the whole car rocks with the power impulses of the 4 great cylinders but the engine is surprisingly quiet, in spite of all those exposed gears and pushrods. The sensation on moving off is quite unlike that given by any other car. The torque is immense, with the engine turning so slowly that the power impulse of each individual cylinder can be felt, but the acceleration is impressive nevertheless.

The straight-toothed pinions of the gearbox are quieter than would be expected, producing a gentle hum of fairly high pitch. When the engine is given full throttle, the gears emit a delighted yelp at each firing impulse, which I can only render as 'yip-yip-yip-yip!'

One probably changes up at about 800 rpm in normal driving and above the peak revs of 1,200 rpm the engine suddenly becomes rough and noisy – its charm is its massive torque and it prefers not to rev too highly.

The gearbox is superb, nay, sublime. It has straight-toothed sliding pinions, with no form of synchronization, of course. Yet the changes, up or down, can be as fast as the driver wishes or more leisurely, with no sound or shock. The gearlever and clutch pedal are both light in action and one cannot imagine a better gearchange. While the engine is reasonably flexible, it has a fairly restricted rev range and so the gearlever is quite busy on a journey, which is far from being a hardship with such a perfect change. Top gear is so high that the engine appears to be idling at 50 mph.

Though the driver sits very high, the centre of gravity of the car is reasonably low and it corners with little roll. It is well balanced and feels quite small and manageable, nipping round the curves in a most satisfactory manner. Should the rear end start to break away, the steering is high-geared for instant correction. Unfortunately, the steering is also exceedingly heavy, which is rather unexpected with such narrow tyres.

Let us forget its trivial faults, though. Even now this is a great car, and in 1903 it must have been beyond belief. The sheer sensation of unleashing that giant power is magnificent and, as the gale of wind that tries to tear you from your lofty seat becomes ever stronger, the narrow tyres skim the surface of the road as their axles dance on undamped springs. There is a deep mutter from the exhaust, the high note of the gears rises higher and higher – 'yip-yip-yip-yip' – and the thrash of the chains can be heard behind you. Nobody has ever driven as fast as this before and you are a god among men, singing exultantly at the top of your voice, crouching over the wheel to cleave the wind, willing this marvellous machine to go faster, faster, faster.

After driving a car like this, I can understand the obsession of the early motorists with speed, reprehensible though it was. To drive at 160 mph in a Ferrari is a mere pub-crawl in comparison. There is little sensation of speed, the huge tyres are glued to the road, and you can stop in a few moments with a touch of the right toe. At less than half this speed in the Sixty, you are battling with the elements, and while the dusty macadam seems to become as narrow as a plank, you are staying alive because your skill and the strength of your arms are alone keeping this wayward monster from dashing itself to pieces against the trees. It is not frightening, because you are drunk with the sheer exhilaration of it, and if you want to stop, the power of both feet and your strong right arm can rein in your steed before you reach the horizon.

But don't stop, just go on and on, faster and ever faster, until not a drop of petrol remains in the tank!

The Sixty was the top car in an age when men regarded motoring as a pretty virile sport. Like steeplechasing – 'the image of war and only five and twenty per cent of the danger' – they preferred the games in which one risked one's neck. Yet there was one man who bought a Sixty, loved it so that he kept it for the rest of his life, yet was honest enough to write disparagingly of it because it was not really practical. The man was Alfred C. Harmsworth, later Lord Northcliffe, and here are his words:

Though I am the possessor of one of the most powerful motorcars in England, I am not at all an admirer of them for ordinary use ... I consider that these heavy and powerful road engines are a mere passing freak of the hour.

Their weight makes them comfortable on rough roads, but the amount of petrol required to drive them is a serious item of expense. So far as this country is concerned, there are very few roads on which they can, so to speak, be let loose. On the long, straight roads of France, it is pleasant to indulge in a sixty miles an hour spin now and then, but when one considers the rapidity with which these monsters consume tyres, the fact that they are not at all suited to the conveyance of ladies, and are most uncomfortable on wet, windy, or dusty days, I am inclined to think that a few years will see their disappearance.

Harmsworth was before his time in advocating closed coachwork for almost every type of car, a state of affairs which was not to be realized for over 30 years. In the early Edwardian era, most closed cars were town carriages with landaulette or limousine bodies. A landaulette had leather rear quarters, which could be folded to permit the occupants the benefit of fresh air in fine weather, while a limousine had a solid roof, but in either case there was a glass division behind the driver and his compartment had no side windows.

Alfred Harmsworth, later Lord Northcliffe, in his 1902 40 hp Mercédès, which he replaced with a 1903 60 hp model.

Such cars were invariably driven by 'shuvvers' – it was 'bad form' to pronounce foreign words correctly and chauffeur was a French word. A gentleman could never be seen driving such a car, because it was 'not done' or 'not quite the thing'. In many families, the master drove a powerful open touring car and the chauffeur would have been outraged if his employer had dared to take the wheel of 'his' closed car. The exception was the 2-seater drophead-coupé – often called a doctor's coupé – which was an owner-driver's car. Subsequently, the enclosed-drive limousine arrived and could equally well be driven by the owner or his paid driver.

Up to 1906 or so, it was most unusual to mount an enclosed body on a powerful chassis. A medium-sized car usually had better manners in traffic and high speed was not required, as town cars were seldom used for touring. It was considered that a landaulette or limousine body would eventually be spoilt if used constantly for fast runs on indifferent country roads, for once a coachbuilt body started to rattle it was almost impossible to cure it.

Similarly, the very big 4-cylinder engines of high-speed cars tended to shake and twist the body unmercifully when idling. Such firms as Mercédès and Panhard et Levassor made medium-sized chassis especially suitable for closed coachwork and Renault were very successful in this field. An engine of 3 litres or a little larger would idle much more smoothly than a powerful monster and shaft drive was preferred to chains, because they tended to obstruct the side doors.

As we shall see in the next chapter, the closed body began to invade the domain of the super cars when the 6-cylinder engine became practical. There was a long war between the chassis manufacturers and the coachbuilders, for while the former complained that the bodies were much too heavy, the latter grumbled that chassis were far too flexible. There was truth in both these assertions, for unnecessary weight killed performance and was hard on tyres, while a whippy frame could strain the joints and crack the panels of the coachwork.

Although the appearance of closed bodies did not alter greatly for several years, there were unseen developments which were very important. These included the provision of a sub-frame, on which the body was built, with a flexible mounting that allowed the chassis to whip without twisting the coachwork. The sub-frame was sometimes supplied by the car manufacturer, notably by the British Daimler Company. Ash, a light wood, was increasingly used for the body framework, while metal panels, often aluminium, replaced the heavier mahogany.

Another problem was the very high roof-line, on which so many purchasers insisted. It was necessary to provide plenty of clearance for the top hats which men wore, while the millinery of the ladies could be pretty lofty, too. These high bodies rolled excessively, especially as there were complaints if the springs were stiffened to give some sort of stability. To drive the high closed cars of this period is pretty hard work, for corners must be taken very steadily

The first closed cars were almost invariably chauffeur-driven, the owner of this Renault probably driving an open Mercédès himself.

and a sudden gust of wind can cause a nasty swerve. This was a further reason why the master was seldom tempted to take his servant's place behind the wheel.

The 1903–6 period might well be regarded as the adolescence of motoring. Cars suddenly became fast enough to be fun and some of their drivers were like naughty little boys, showing off disgracefully and thumbing their noses at authority. There is a curious parallel with the present day, when the imposition of unprecedented motoring restrictions is being answered by the production of faster and yet faster cars. Men who appear to be in their right minds are paying almost unimaginable sums for vehicles that can only land them in prison if they ever use their full performance. Let us bear this in mind before we utterly condemn those courageous young men who squandered their patrimony on 60 hp Mercédès and disappeared in a cloud of dust.

The Upper Crust

COLOUR ILLUSTRATIONS

OPPOSITE
A Panhard et Levassor racing car, depicted on
the ancient coloured tiles at the Michelin building.

PAGES 66–7
The London-Edinburgh was the high-performance version of the Rolls-Royce
Silver Ghost. This is Peter Hampton's very sporting open 4-seater.

PAGE 68
The incomparable 60 hp Mercédès of 1903. 'Nobody has ever driven
as fast as this before and you are a god among men . . .'

ARIS AMSTERDAM 1898   CHARRON sur PANHARD

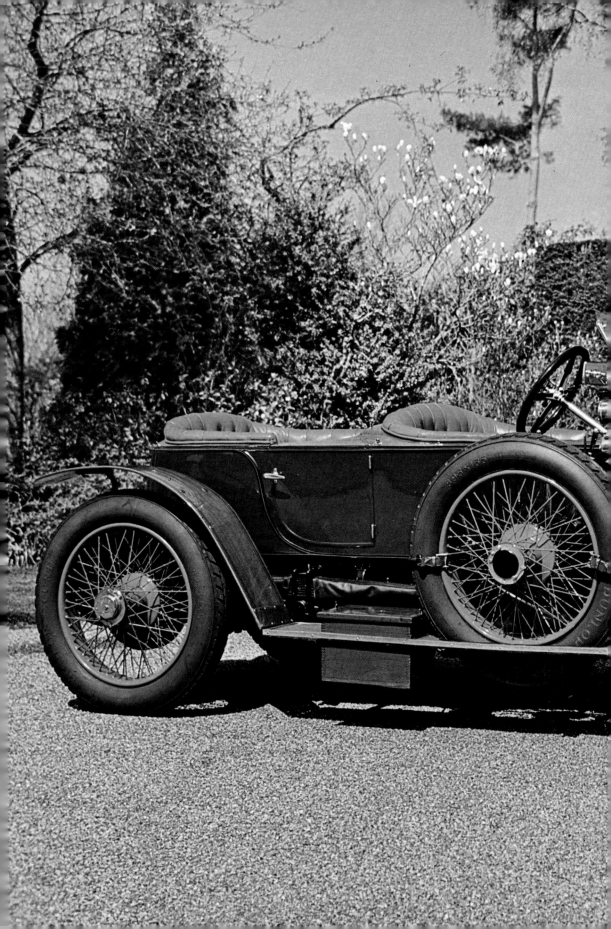

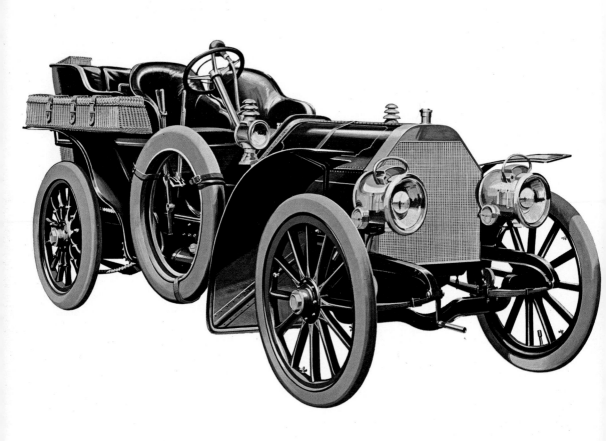

RENAULT
La 40 cv Sport

COLOUR ILLUSTRATIONS

PAGE 69

The Renault 40 cv sport was one of the most spectacular cars
ever built, though it had the reputation of being a man-killer.
This is a Renault advertising poster of the early 1920s.

PAGE 70

This 6½-litre 6-cylinder Hispano-Suiza had its body built by Kellner to the
order of an Indian Maharajah; it now lives in the Stratford Museum.

PAGE 71

One of the best-looking cars of all time, the Continental version
of the Rolls-Royce Phantom II was ideal for long-distance touring.

OPPOSITE ABOVE

A Packard Twelve town car with coachwork by Le Baron.

OPPOSITE BELOW

The Rolls-Royce Camargue is for the man who regards driving
as an art and enjoys it too much to employ a chauffeur.

4
The Silver Ghost
1907-1914

A 1909 Rolls-Royce Silver Ghost with a landaulette body, which was typical of chauffeur-driven coachwork and did not alter appreciably for many years. The electric lights cost about £75 extra.

he adolescence of motoring was soon over. When speed was a novelty it was perhaps understandable that drivers made excessive use of it. Very quickly, they discovered that the roads at the beginning of the century formed extremely poor race tracks. Especially in England sharp corners, often blind and deceptive, abounded, while steep hills and dangerous crossroads were everywhere. To travel fast on the narrow, winding roads was a perilous adventure.

The unexpected might be found round any corner, such as a horse-drawn vehicle guided only by the quadruped while the man slept on the hay. Even the rule of the road was not universally practised, carts or bicycles often pulling over to the wrong side when met. In villages, conversations took place in the middle of the street, while any tree or bush might be concealing the local bobby with his stopwatch, avid to trap the speeding motorist.

Though cars with powerful engines were now available, they still needed plenty of space in which to stop. Brakes only operated on the rear wheels, which would lock and skid without giving much retardation. The 'dreaded sideslip' was a very real danger, for few tyres had an effective non-skid tread pattern and some road surfaces were almost unimaginably slippery. The wood block roads, particularly common in London, became soaked with axle grease and the urine of horses, which after a shower of rain combined to form a coating more perilous than black ice. Steel-studded tyres were sold to combat this condition and became compulsory wear for London taxis, on one front and one rear wheel diagonally.

The man who drove fast soon grew tired of a series of 'close shaves' and 'narrow squeaks', gradually adopting a less frenzied pace. Furthermore, there was a social deterrent, the driver who habitually frightened his neighbours into the ditch being labelled road hog in England or *pas sérieux*, that most damning epithet, in France. He was quickly 'dropped', which meant that neither he nor his family received any more invitations. This was a thing that nobody would risk, for although the Edwardian era was wonderfully gay and light-hearted, people relied on each other for entertainment; a family that had received the cold shoulder could be terribly lonely.

This complete renunciation of the joys of speed had been brought about, more than anything, by the Paris–Madrid race. Owing to the greatly increased power of the cars, coupled with the total impossibility of controlling the crowds of spectators on such a long route, there were many serious accidents and the race was stopped at Bordeaux. Conditioned by 2 appalling world wars, we are now so callous that such an event would not shock us. In 1903 the newspapers in every country had banner headlines about 'the race to death' and readers were aghast. For the first time, the public had it brought home to them that fast cars could be really deadly.

More than half a century later, the Le Mans disaster killed ten times as many people as had died in Paris–Madrid. Yet the wave of horror was far less, which shows how lightly we now value human

'With constabulary duties to
be done, to be done,
A policeman's lot is not a
happy one, happy one.'

–A contemporary impression
of an early speed trap.

life. In the sunshine of the early 1900s, when peace and prosperity seemed likely to last for ever, Paris–Madrid was a holocaust which shook the world. From being fun, speed suddenly became wicked and no motor manufacturer dared to mention a car's performance in his advertising.

The new craze was for silence, a quality which the vendors of the noisiest little cars unblushingly claimed. Nevertheless, some of the great cars of the Edwardian era were quieter than anything that is made today. The demand for silence was a sensible one but simultaneously a new craving appeared which was not. This was the obsession with going everywhere in top gear, which resulted in some very bad driving habits being formed, as well as some rather horrible cars being built. Instead of making their gearboxes quieter and easier to handle, manufacturers claimed in their advertisements that their cars had climbed this or that hill in top gear. The sound of knocking engines and the smell of burning clutches proved that far too many people were adopting this destructive method of driving.

The answer to these demands for silence and flexibility proved to be the 6-cylinder engine. The straight-six, with its near-perfect balance and overlapping power impulses, had all the necessary qualities, but designers were horrified to find that there were formidable difficulties. In those spacious days, engines were built long because the cylinders were cast separately or in pairs and lengthy crankshaft bearings were thought to be necessary. The paramount necessity for rigidity was not yet understood and the

Some motorists were genuinely ashamed of the nuisance they caused by dust and this Hotchkiss is fitted with various palliatives to avoid sucking up the top surface of the macadam.

engineers were appalled when torsional vibrations, so violent that the crankshaft often broke in two, occurred as soon as the engine was revved up. In brief, these long cranks wound up and unwound like a spring when a certain critical speed was reached.

Many firms, rushing precipitately into the manufacture of 6-cylinder cars, had to scrap them and return red-faced to their 4-cylinder models. Even Mercédès, who had made the world's best 4-cylinder car, built some mediocre sixes and lost their leadership. Curiously archaic monsters of 120 × 140 mm (9,504 cc) and 120 × 150 mm (10,183 cc), these cars were lorry-like in their handling and had none of the charm of the immortal Sixty.

To make the crankshafts more rigid, shorter engines had to be built. The crankshaft journals were unavoidably shortened and their diameter also had to be increased, which greatly improved the torsional rigidity. However, this meant more heavily loaded main bearings with a higher rubbing speed. With lubrication by drip feed and splash, bearing troubles were inevitable. It entailed the adoption of the full pressure oiling system, which is used on all cars today, but there were quite a few problems to be solved before that could be made to work properly.

Frederick Henry Royce (later Sir Henry) who designed and built 'the Best Car in the World'.

It was found that more pressure was necessary to gain full oil circulation through the crankshaft than had been imagined, because of centrifugal force. Having overcome that, the oil-throw from the big-ends was greatly increased, which over-lubricated the pistons and formed carbon in the combustion chambers. In the absence of modern slotted scraper rings, baffles were usually placed beneath the cylinder bores, with slots just wide enough to allow the connecting rods to pass through them, which were effective but made assembly much more difficult.

The above paragraphs over-simplify the very real engineering problems that had to be overcome. There were some firms that soldiered on with whippy crankshafts and splash lubrication. They restricted the breathing of their engines with tortuous manifolds and small carburettors, which discouraged drivers from reaching the higher revolutions, where lurked the fearful torsional vibration and the broken crankshaft. Such 6-cylinder engines could be silent and flexible but they were deadly dull to drive and desperately fragile if accidentally over-revved downhill.

Yet there was a considerable demand for a 6-cylinder car to replace the 4-cylinder Mercédès. At this precise moment, a car was produced which was so outstanding that its makers were soon daring to advertise it as 'The Best Car in the World'. It was, of course, the Rolls-Royce Silver Ghost.

Henry Royce had already designed a 10 hp 2-cylinder car, a 15 hp 3-cylinder, and a 20 hp 4-cylinder. These models had appeared in quick succession and had all been equally successful. He then built a 30 hp 6-cylinder luxury car, which had all the prevailing crankshaft problems. With cylinders cast in pairs and splash lubrication, it was entitled to be a flop, and it was.

Luckily only half a dozen cars had been built when the first crank

The Silver Ghost, the actual 1907 40/50 hp car after which all side-valve Rolls-Royces were unofficially named.
The property of Rolls-Royce Motors, it is, of course, still in perfect running order.

broke, but there had been so much publicity that the model could not be withdrawn without losing face disastrously. In a crash test programme, Royce worked day and night and evolved various palliatives, such as lightening the crankshaft mass by removing balance weights, lightening the auxiliary front flywheel and, for the next batch of cars, increasing the diameter of the main bearing journals and fitting much lighter connecting rods.

The 30 hp was saved and 37 were actually sold, but to that incredible engineer it was dead. Within 6 months, his entirely new car was designed and built! It appeared at the 1906 motor show and deliveries began early in 1907. This was to be the most famous car of all time, the 40/50 hp Rolls-Royce, soon to be called the Silver Ghost from the pet-name of one of the earliest examples.

In the Ghost, Royce shortened his engine by having the cylinders cast in blocks of 3. It would probably have been possible, even then, to cast a monobloc of this size, but it would have been extremely awkward to machine, so this was the best solution. Full pressure lubrication was adopted, with crankshaft journals which were of large diameter for the period.

The side-valves were operated from a single camshaft, the overhead inlet valves of Royce's earlier designs having been deleted. In addition to the trembler coil ignition of Rolls-Royce manufacture, a Bosch high-tension magneto was added, plus a little friction brake to ensure that the intermittent load, caused by the armature passing through the magnetic field, did not cause a faint chattering of the timing gears. The magneto had a superior high-speed performance but the trembler coil gave very easy starting.

When warm, the engine can be started 9 times out of 10 by merely switching on the ignition, the petrol vapour remaining in the cylinders for a couple of hours. When cold, one floods the carburettor and pulls the handle over a few times in leisurely fashion with the ignition switched off; a touch of the switch then sets the engine going. Though the early Silver Ghosts had no starters, there was no need to retain a muscular servant, and a lady driver would not find the starting routine arduous.

The Ghost had the usual cone clutch of the period and a 4-speed gearbox with a direct third and overdrive fourth speed. The overdrive was soon deleted, partly because it made an audible whine but principally, I feel, in deference to the universal habit of driving all day in top; 3-speed gearboxes were preferred by most drivers and the Sheffield-Simplex was sold as a single-geared car, though it actually had a little 2-speed box tucked away in case one got stuck on a hill.

The gearchange was the worst feature of the Ghost, demanding considerable skill if really silent changes were to be ensured. As the right-hand lever was moved to the end of one of the slots in the gate, it would pivot sideways and lock itself by entering a suitably shaped notch. On making the next change, one had to remember to unlock the lever before unslotting it, which seemed a needless complication.

The orthodox channel-section chassis rode on semi-elliptic

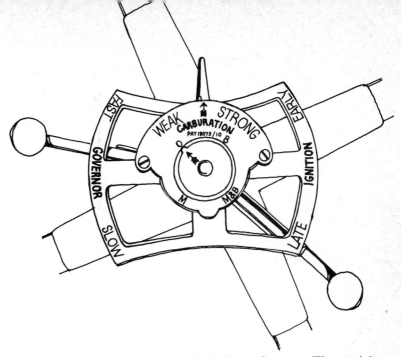

The controls above the steering wheel of the Rolls-Royce Silver Ghost. The central knob switched on the dual ignition by magneto and battery, the short lever controlled the two variable carburettor jets, that on the right set the timing of both ignitions, while the left one influenced the throttle governor.

springs in front, the axle being brakeless, of course. The straight-bevel rear axle was silent because a fitter was allowed up to a fortnight to obtain a perfect meshing of the crown-wheel and pinion. It was located on 2 trailing radius arms and a central tubular torque frame, all of which required a lot of greasing points for the many ball joints, but the excellence of the roadholding made this worthwhile. Later a conventional torque tube greatly reduced the chauffeur's chores but the roadholding was not quite so exceptional. At first 2 semi-elliptic springs were united at their rear ends by a centrally mounted platform spring, subsequently replaced by three-quarter elliptics, and finally by the fashionable cantilevers.

Braking, as was normal in those days, was by a hand brake func-

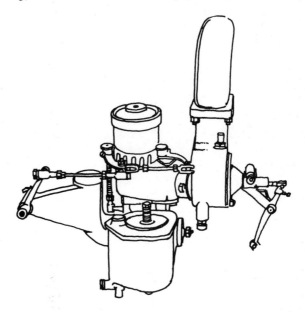

The carburettor of the Rolls-Royce Silver Ghost had two variable jets and an automatic air valve. As it was designed by F.H. Royce, it is not surprising that it had to be meticulously constructed but would last for ever once it was properly tuned.

tioning in rear wheel drums and a foot-operated transmission brake behind the gearbox. The first Ghosts had an engine of 114×114 mm (7,036 cc), increased to 114×121 mm (7,428 cc) in 1909. This brought the power output up from 48 to over 60 bhp and the London–Edinburgh version probably developed 75 bhp.

As to performance, I have a 1911 short-chassis open touring car, which I have timed at 71 mph, and the sporting London–Edinburgh type was officially timed at 78 mph at Brooklands. The steering and roadholding are remarkably good, even by modern standards, and the ride is surprisingly comfortable, in spite of the narrow tyres. As with any 2-wheel braking system, the retardation is somewhat gradual, but it was up to the average in its day.

I have made many long journeys in this car, in England and Scotland as well as on the Continent. My best petrol consumption is 15 mpg but 13 mpg is more normal. It is the sensation of gliding in almost complete silence that puts the Silver Ghost above other cars of its era, but it also seems virtually immune from normal wear and tear. I have owned later Rolls-Royces which I liked rather less, in spite of their better brakes. Most of the last Ghosts had huge coachbuilt bodies and were too big and heavy to be much fun to drive. However, that was after the period covered by this chapter.

To the engineer, this chassis is still a poem in metal, without an

A 1910 Rolls-Royce Silver Ghost with Rudge-Whitworth detachable wire wheels and the parallel-sided bonnet, which some customers preferred to the later, tapered type.

ounce of surplus weight in any part of it. It was designed by a genius who reached heights of inspiration which perhaps he never quite touched again.

In trying to produce the car of all cars, which will be preferred by the upper crust, too many motor manufacturers give birth to monsters. History proves that these white elephants are never successful, even the wealthiest buyers preferring something that can be parked without embarrassment and driven by people of average skill, who have not been trained to handle an omnibus. Yet, several of the great Continental *marques* introduced huge 6-cylinder cars, in addition to the unwieldy Mercédès already mentioned.

Fiat made a real giant of 11,039 cc which had chain drive, as was usual with the monsters. At least it boasted a compressed-air starting system, operating at very high pressure, and the brakes were water-cooled – no doubt this was most necessary when descending an Alp. Lorraine-Dietrich (formerly De Dietrich), who built some of the largest 4-cylinder racing cars, went all out for the upper-crust market with a gigantic 6-cylinder of 11,951 cc. Perhaps it is a little ominous that both these firms offered alternative 4-cylinder engines of 10,563 cc and 12,058 cc respectively. By comparison, the Mors six was almost reasonable with only 9,190 cc, but there were other monsters of less reputed makes.

Apart from their impractical aspects, there were remarkably few people who could comfortably afford to buy and run these larger than lifesize vehicles. There was, and I think still is, a delusion that there were a great many wealthy men in the Edwardian era. Certainly this was far from being the case in England, but there was a general appearance of affluence which was totally false.

There were many men who lived the lives of country gentlemen, in tolerable style with several servants, and they were locally thought to be rich. Yet most of them did it on an income of less than £10 a week, which was possible because the cost of living was so low and taxation was negligible. In 1901 fewer than a million people paid any income tax at all in the British Isles and only 400,000 earned or received over £400 a year.

In Edwardian times, things had changed remarkably little from those long ago days before Queen Victoria ascended the throne; everybody spent what money he could get and those less fortunate were reduced to charity. There were virtually no bureaucrats to support, but few Englishmen became really rich. Manufacturing methods relied on the skilled hand work of individuals and agriculture was still the husbandry of the middle ages in essentials. If there were any millionaires in England, they had come from the USA or South Africa.

Furthermore, it was generally believed that the British aristocracy were wealthy, but that was far from true, and most of them were already finding it hard to make ends meet. Charles Rolls, who moved in upper-class circles, was fully aware of this, and it was he who insisted that the Best Car in the World should be neither too large nor too costly. An engine of 7 litres was only medium-sized in

85

those days but if it was efficient it could ensure ample performance, provided that a stern hand was kept on the coachbuilders, who always tended to build too big and too heavy.

So the Silver Ghost was the right size and its chassis price was less than £1000. The purchaser often had his pet coachbuilder and he chose all his own accessories, but a complete car, ready for the road, might cost £1200 for an open tourer or £1400 for a chauffeur-driven landaulette or limousine. The Hon Charles was right, for although there were few men who could have paid much more, there were enough with that sort of money to buy all the cars that Henry Royce could make.

The Rolls-Royce was desired for many reasons, but its appearance was one of the most important. That wonderful radiator shape and the long, low bonnet with its evenly spaced rivets were all part of the character of a car that looked a thoroughbred in every line. It had an air of lightness about it that made its competitors look heavy and plebeian. It was soon accepted, almost all over the world, as being the best that money could buy, though it was far from being the most expensive car, or the largest.

This approval was not unanimous, however, for the French had their own contender. There are still Frenchmen who think that the 6-cylinder Delaunay-Belleville was a better car than the Rolls-Royce, or at least just as good. This is a fascinating subject for discussion which will probably never reach any conclusion because the cars, and the thinking behind them, were so very different.

I am a tremendous admirer of the pre-1914 Delaunay-Bellevilles, but because I am a Rolls-Royce owner I might be accused of prejudice. I therefore wrote to my friend, Serge Pozzoli, who is perhaps the foremost French motoring historian, for his views on this problem. Here is a translation of his reply:

In 1870, France had lost an important war and Alsace Lorraine. As the expansion of Japan proves today, lost wars force countries to work hard, and in 1900 France was not only very rich but one of the greatest industrial nations (if not the greatest of all).

The Delaunay-Belleville factories were specialists in steam machinery, which they sold all over the world, and the name was therefore known by world industrialists as a synonym of high quality. When Delaunay-Belleville put cars upon the market, the firm concentrated on luxury vehicles. From 1908 to 1914, the wealthiest men in the world (including Englishmen) bought Delaunay-Bellevilles, Rolls being a name known for only a short time. It was naturally in England that the name of Rolls first reached the top, but world buyers who had heard of it were tending to class it as a make with too sporting an image. One could say that in 1912 80 per cent of people regarded Delaunay-Belleville as the leading *marque* in the world.

Was it better than a Rolls? I do not believe so because the firm, unlike that at Derby, dispersed its efforts in making too many different models.

That seems a very fair summary and I do not propose to take sides. The suggestion that Rolls-Royce actually lost sales by too much competition activity is interesting and I suppose that such things as

86

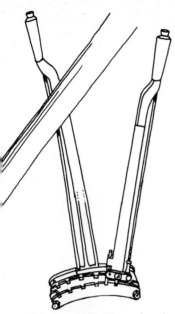

Delaunay-Belleville continued to use the quadrant gearchange for many years after other manufacturers had rushed to copy the Mercédès gate change. Here the lever is in the neutral position between first and reverse.

the top-gear run from London to Edinburgh, the TT victory, and the Alpine Trials, tended to give the car a sporting background that would be distasteful to the ultra-conservative. Certainly, it would have been unthinkable for Delaunay-Belleville to have taken part in such demonstrations and Rolls-Royce adopted the same attitude after they had really arrived.

It is beyond any argument that Delaunay-Belleville made superb steam engines and when they became car manufacturers the same standard of engineering was maintained. Both Delaunays and Rolls were built with similar skill and care and their engineering was of such painstaking perfection that no firm could approach it now without going bankrupt. The Delaunay-Belleville steam engines had had fully forced lubrication through drilled crankshafts, since well back into the old century, the firm holding a master patent for this arrangement.

It was natural that even the first Delaunay-Belleville cars of 1904 had forced lubrication, using an eccentric-driven plunger pump as was steam-engine practice. Like Panhard, Delaunay-Belleville were very conservative in technical matters, retaining the quadrant gearchange for many years after Mercédès had made the gate change fashionable. Similarly, their larger cars had chain drive right up to 1911. Nevertheless, their advanced lubrication system stood them in good stead when they started making 6-cylinder cars in 1908, for they seem to have avoided the crankshaft problems that gave other engineers so many sleepless nights.

Six-cylinder Delaunays ranged in size from $2\frac{1}{2}$ litres to 9 litres. At first their design varied enormously from model to model, some having 6 separate cylinder castings, others 3 blocks of 2, and the smallest six was actually a monobloc as early as 1908. Gradually they went over to 2 blocks of 3, like the Rolls-Royce, for the larger models. Some of the smaller sixes only had 3 main crankshaft bearings but the bigger ones had 7, again like the Rolls.

Delaunay-Bellevilles had cast-iron cylinders with fixed heads on aluminium crank-cases. They had side-valves, which were inclined to give more compact combustion chambers from 1912 onwards, and beautiful tubular connecting rods. In the period with which we are dealing, from 1908 to 1914 inclusive, there was a marked tendency to lengthen the piston stroke of successive Delaunay-Belleville models, which must have posed serious crankshaft design problems. Presumably Delaunay had so completely licked the torsional vibration bogey that they dared use these very long strokes in 6-cylinder engines, though such dimensions were normally confined to 4-cylinder racing cars.

The 40 hp Delaunay-Belleville of 1908 had a bore and stroke of 115 × 130 mm (8,102 cc) and in 1911 it grew into the 45 hp of 115 × 150 mm (9,348 cc). This was replaced by an entirely new model in 1914, the 45/50, of 103 × 160 mm (7,999 cc), perhaps the finest Delaunay of them all. It must be admitted that the great firm at St Denis also built monsters, but only 3 of them, one in 1908 and 2 in 1909, and they were for a very special customer.

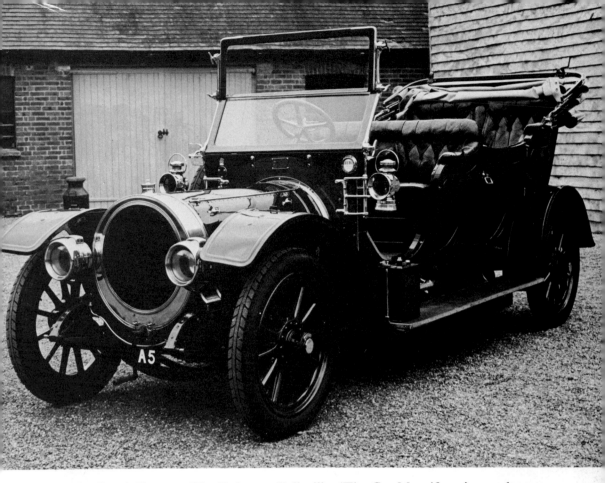

The Delaunay-Belleville, 'The Car Magnificent', was the preferred automobile of kings, emperors, and heads of state; incidentally, Queen Victoria's yacht had Delaunay-Belleville boilers. Among the most devoted enthusiasts for these great cars was the Czar of all the Russias and it was he who asked M. Delaunay-Belleville to build him the most magnificent cars of all. These huge machines had 6-cylinder engines of 134×140 mm (11,851 cc) and were fitted with vast bodies of the utmost luxury.

In order to produce engines of this size, the designers harked back to the old 40 hp 4-cylinder Delaunay of 7,901 cc, of which production had ceased when the 6-cylinder models were introduced. This old vehicle had had 4 separate cylinders of 134 mm bore, so 6 of them were mounted on a new crank-case and, hey-presto, the Czar had his mighty engine. The chassis followed normal Delaunay-Belleville practice, with chain drive and 2 water-cooled transmission brakes.

His Majesty's cars were fitted with compressed-air starters. These were sufficiently powerful to start the immensely heavy vehicles in gear, thanks to very large air containers charged at extremely high pressure. This instant and silent getaway was most impressive, but the main object was to avoid assassination, the moment of departure being always a time of danger. Subsequently, a less powerful compressed-air starter was offered on the standard 6-cylinder models, the air motor driving the front of the crankshaft

'The Car Magnificent': The Delaunay-Belleville was considered by many Frenchmen to be even better than the Silver Ghost. The round radiator and bonnet shape may have been inspired by the steam boilers with which the great French firm made their name, but in any case it was extremely handsome. This one has open coachwork by Mulliners of Birmingham and belongs to Chris Jaques.

OVERLEAF His Imperial Majesty the Czar of all the Russias, with his family in his 12-litre 6-cylinder Delaunay-Belleville, of which he had three. The rear wheels were fitted with twin tyres and the drive was by chains.

89

The 6-cylinder T-head
Delaunay-Belleville engine,
as used in the cars of the
Czar. The finned casing
behind the radiator contains
the air compressor for
self-starting.

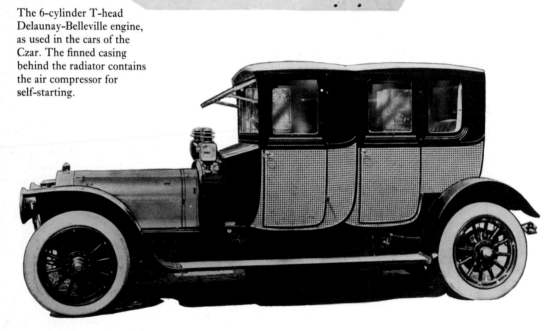

A glorious enclosed-drive
limousine by Labourdette,
with canework finish to body
panels, on a 1912 6½-litre
Delaunay-Belleville chassis.

and acting as a pump when the engine was running. A starting
handle could still be attached at the front of the machine if necessary.
The whole outfit was heavy and took up a lot of space, so it was
dropped without regret when a reliable electric starter became
available in 1914.

No ugly car has ever reached the top and the Delaunay-Belleville
had a patrician elegance that has never been surpassed. The best
coachbuilders loved to create bodies on Delaunays because that
great circular radiator and bonnet – inspired, it was said, by the
shape of a steam boiler – was the ideal beginning for the coachwork
of the epoch. It was to suit later body styles less well, but at a time
when the ideal was a long, low bonnet, followed by elaborate
carriagework rising tier upon tier, the round Delaunay radiator

Delaunay-Belleville pioneered full pressure lubrication, so the usual dashboard-mounted oil tanks were not required and the petrol tank took their place, of which the filler cap can be seen on top.

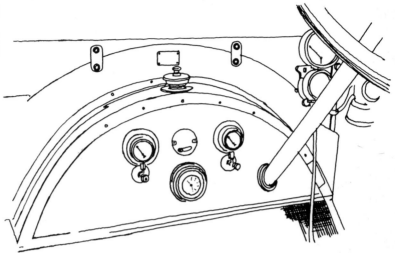

The small handle on the right is pulled out to slide the camshaft, thus engaging the half-compression cams for easy cranking.

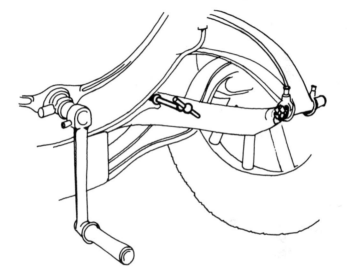

The rear platform springing of the Delaunay-Belleville, consisting of a transverse leaf spring shackled to two semi-elliptics, all in leather gaiters.

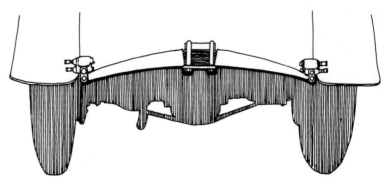

was just right. The bonnet blended into a dashboard-mounted petrol tank, which occupied space that was required on other cars for oil tanks and drip feeds. The oil stayed in the sump, as in modern cars, and the Delaunay-Belleville driver was free from the usual spots of lubricant on coat and gloves.

Of the 3,754 6-cylinder Delaunays produced from 1908 to 1914, only 138 were the great 8/9-litre models, 524 were 6½-litre cars, and 2,508 were of the popular 4/4½-litre size. From 1907 to 1914, Rolls-Royce made only one model of 7/7½-litre capacity. Well over 3000 were manufactured during that period, so the British firm were far more successful in selling powerful cars than their French rivals, even if their total sales were a little less. Yet the Delaunay, rather than the Rolls, was the car of kings, largely because British monarchs favoured the Daimler and remained faithful to the Coventry firm for more than 50 years.

It is curious that the Daimler of that era appealed to King Edward, for it was a big 4-cylinder chain-driven machine of considerable performance and little refinement. A 38 hp Daimler won the first Shelsley Walsh hillclimb in 1905 and these cars were the most successful in the popular hillclimbs held, with police co-operation, on public roads. This form of sport, curiously enough, did not attract the public odium of racing, because most cars climbed pretty slowly, anyway. In 1906 the biggest Daimler was a 4-cylinder of 10,604 cc, and fairly crude it was, too.

Daimler were only too well aware that their cars were not in the same world as the Silver Ghost and were terrified that royalty would change their allegiance. Accordingly, a batch of 6-cylinder cars was hurriedly put in hand, but when they were completed it was found that they were totally unsaleable, for once again frightful torsional vibrations threatened to break the crankshafts in twain.

Desperate measures were called for and that brilliant genius, Mr (later Dr) Frederick Lanchester, was approached. Lanchester was perpetually in dispute with the directors of the firm which bore his name and was gradually handing over the design side to his brother George, while he pursued an independent course. He worked at first for Daimler almost in secret, but at the beginning of 1909 his position of Consulting Engineer to the company was made official. He got them off the hook remarkably quickly by inventing the slipper-flywheel vibration damper, which is still found in the majority of in-line 6-cylinder engines, often in its modern form with bonded rubber instead of a friction clutch.

Royce applied the slipper-flywheel damper to the crankshaft of the Silver Ghost in 1911, permitting more power to be obtained without spoiling the legendary smoothness. There was some controversy about this and it was suggested that both great men had hit upon the same solution simultaneously. Nevertheless, it was Lanchester who patented it and to him must go the credit.

At this time, the Daimler Company wished to abandon chain drive, which was regarded as being old-fashioned, and bevel-driven axles were to be used. It was Dr Lanchester who persuaded them to

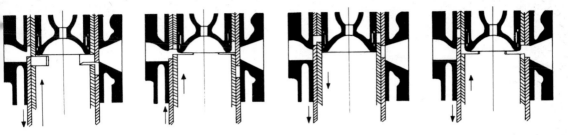

The movement of the twin sleeves in a Daimler Silent Knight engine.

adopt his own special form of worm gear instead, which became an important feature of the cars because it lowered the driveshaft by some 6 ins, permitting a flat floor to be used with no central hump.

A much more radical change in 1909 was the decision to use sleeve-valve engines in all future Daimler models. Most Edwardian engines made a hearty clatter with their poppet-valves, tappets, camshafts, and timing gears. The Knight engine eliminated all these things, the valves consisting of a pair of sleeves surrounding each piston, with ports cut in them to correspond with those in the cylinder walls. A very small crankshaft with half-inch throws moved the sleeves up and down for an inch or so, the drive being by a silent chain.

Fundamentally, the sleeves were silent in operation, but by minute attention to detail and superb workmanship, Royce was able to make a poppet-valve engine which was just as quiet. Almost arrogantly, he left his valves to operate in the open when nearly all other designers were endeavouring to reduce the clatter by using sound-deadening valve covers.

Using their new Silent Knight power units, Daimler introduced a full range of luxury cars, headed by a huge 57·2 hp 6-cylinder chassis with engine dimensions of 124 × 130 mm (9,421 cc). Daimler cars were always incredibly cheap for their size and this great machine cost only £900, less body. King George V adored the 57·2 hp model, of which he had a fleet of limousines, landaulettes, and shooting brakes. Indeed, when they had long been out of production, he commanded Daimler to build him some new cars, but using 57·2 hp engines to the ancient design.

The biggest Daimler was almost exclusively a royal car, the 38 hp model of 6,252 cc being large enough for most purchasers, with its 11 ft 6 ins wheelbase. There were smaller-engined cars, but though these were ideal town carriages for milady, their performance, or lack of it, was pretty lamentable. Many writers tend to dismiss the sleeve-valve Daimlers as being dull and uninteresting. This they were emphatically not, and in the hands of an intelligent chauffeur, who was versed in their ways, they were utterly reliable and lasted for ever. Moreover, few chassis have had such superb formal bodywork mounted upon them by the great British coachbuilders.

Among the pomp and circumstance of a great occasion, the Daimler was in its element. For the man who drove himself, however, it was heavy and unresponsive compared with a Silver Ghost. That the Kings of England preferred it to all others may have been because they were seldom tempted to drive their own cars. Far be it

95

from me to criticize their judgement, but the Daimler could be better enjoyed from the veritable drawing room at the rear than from the upright perch of the mere driver in front.

We have spoken of Dr Lanchester and now we must consider how the Lanchester cars stood in upper-crust rating. Lanchester models had previously been rather smaller than those we have been considering but the 6-cylinder 28 hp engine, introduced in 1906, had always been free from crankshaft torsional problems. Dr Lanchester achieved this by deliberately choosing an over-square configuration, for a short-throw crankshaft is much more rigid than one designed for a longer stroke. When he devised the slipper-flywheel damper for Daimler he applied it to the Lanchester engines, which allowed brother George to add an inch to the stroke. This produced an engine of 4·8 litres, which was used in the new 38 hp car of 1910.

The Lanchester had an excellent performance and the suspension was most effective, while the chassis provided a very large platform for luxurious coachwork. However, it did not have quite the effortless gait of its larger-engined rivals and it was not as quiet mechanically as a Rolls, a Delaunay, or a Daimler. If cars of this class had normally been handled by owner-drivers, it would have been a bestseller, for its epicyclic gearchange was foolproof. However, it was up to one's chauffeur to master a difficult gearbox and so this very great advantage was largely ignored.

Lanchester cars had the engine between the driver and front passenger, a logical position, but some prospective customers were put off by the absence of a long and showy bonnet.

The Lanchester of this epoch was hard to sell, because its appearance was too unconventional. This was due to the Lanchester engine position, which placed the power unit between the driver and the front passenger, with the very wide radiator on the front of the short scuttle and no bonnet. Ever since the 60 hp Mercédès, cars had been judged by the length of their noses, and the beautiful lines of the Rolls-Royce and the Delaunay-Belleville depended on their long, low bonnets. It may be illogical to let the engine hog a large part of the chassis space, but the customers wanted long bonnets and they did not like the looks of the Lanchester.

There remains the status of the Napier to consider in relation to the upper crust. Napier made some good cars and some remarkably bad ones, but they were apt to be over-rated because they had a man behind them with a genius for publicity. This was S.F. Edge, who first got himself into the limelight by winning the 1902 Gordon Bennett race and then made sure that he was never out of it. No matter that he had won because everybody else dropped out; to the British public he was 'Mr Motoring'.

This he confirmed by claiming that he could drive a 6-cylinder Napier at a mile a minute for 24 hours, single-handed. This created howls of disbelief, which was exactly what Edge wanted, and people wrote letters to the papers explaining why the feat was impossible. In 1907, before Brooklands track had been officially opened, S.F. Edge took a 60 hp Napier along there for a few practice laps before the attempt and was horrified to find that violent pre-ignition set in after a few miles; on the roads of England, nobody had ever held a Sixty flat out for more than a short burst. Time was short and it looked as though the much advertised performance would not take place; Edge was no technician and he was in despair.

Then one of the Napier mechanics had a brilliant idea. The side-valve engine had fixed cylinder heads, with screw-in caps for fitting and grinding the valves. He reasoned that the caps over the exhaust valves were becoming red hot and he had some hollow caps turned up. Their cavities were connected into the cooling system so that water was circulated through them by the pump. With fingers crossed another test was made, which revealed a complete cure – the attempt was on!

It is history that S.F. Edge drove his Napier for 24 hours single-handed and averaged 65 mph, in spite of some tyre trouble, while 2 other Napiers were not far behind him. The publicity was enormous and Edge made full use of it, both to blow his own trumpet and that of the Napier car.

Edge was quick to seize on the growing influence of the motoring magazines, especially *The Autocar*. The first motor paper was printed before Queen Victoria's reign, for devotees of steam road coaches, and several journals were being published before the turn of the century. Edge did not write well and the public would now know far too much about cars to be influenced by his assertions. In those days, few people understood the technical side and Edge was able to make claims that seem laughable nowadays. His prose could be boring and he kept the correspondence columns filled for week after week, but the virulence of his attacks on his adversaries and his challenges and wagers made everybody read him down to the last line. He was a public hero, so everything he signed was believed, and other manufacturers were terrified of him.

Many 6-cylinder Napiers broke their crankshafts, but S.F. Edge could sell as many as Montague Napier could make. My mother bought a new Napier before I was born and it was a dreadful car. It had mechanical troubles galore and was a martyr to overheating, while it seldom ran for long on all 6 cylinders. Then the paint and varnish started to peel off the *Roi des Belges* body and my mother decided to show it to the great Mr Edge. She waited for some time and then the celebrated personage came down the steps from his office; in total silence and ignoring the owner completely, he stalked once round the car and then returned whence he had come. A few minutes later, a secretary brought a note saying, 'Mrs Bolster may have her Napier repainted by any good coachbuilder of her choice at my expense. S.F. Edge'. Truth compels me to record that she then bought a 4-cylinder Mercédès and lived happily ever after!

Selwyn Francis Edge, a genius for publicity, who made the name of Napier great.

I must admit that I have driven Lord Montagu's 60 hp Napier in modern times and it is a splendid car with about the same performance as a Silver Ghost. However, it is not so refined, while the engine is definitely noisy when idling, so I am not convinced that the Napier was ever in the Rolls or Delaunay class, despite the assertions of S.F. Edge.

I met that gentleman myself, long after his Napier days, but by then he had lost all his fire. His business acumen had deserted him and his considerable fortune had dwindled as a result of some ill-starred ventures. Here was the man the public had adored and that the other motor manufacturers had loved to hate, but in a few years he was almost forgotten. *C'est la vie!*

By 1914, the best cars travelled with scarcely a sound from their engines, their reliability was absolute, and they had as much performance as anybody could use under the prevailing conditions. It was worth buying the best, because these beautiful cars were so much better in every way than smaller and less costly vehicles. Above all, this was the heyday of the great coachbuilders.

Most of the pleasure of owning an upper-crust car came from the knowledge that it was your very own creation. The chassis you could not design yourself, but every detail of the body was chosen by you – its shape, its colour, its upholstery, its lamps, even the dials on the dashboard were to your personal taste. Most people took their friends along on their many visits to the coachbuilders and it was so exciting to see the ugly duckling daily becoming more like a swan. King Edward used to adore the coachbuilding ritual as the royal Daimlers took shape, being most particular that his own seat allowed a dignified entry and exit and gave his loyal subjects a clear view of him as they shouted 'Good old Teddy!'

When a man bought a car of quality, he knew that the chassis had been hand-built by craftsmen with pride in their work. He had seen

A stately 6-cylinder Napier town carriage with coachwork by Barkers. Luggage could conveniently be carried on the flat roof.

more craftsmen doing unbelievably skilled things with wood, metal, and leather, from which a new and gleaming car emerged in all its perfection. However many miles he travelled, his car remained a personal thing, more precious by far than any other and getting better with age, like a pair of hand-made shoes. He did not realize it, but he was probably enjoying his motoring more than anybody ever had, and more than those who came after him ever could, for Armageddon was just round the corner.

A 1908 advertisement for Delaunay-Belleville.

5
Hispano-Suiza
1920-1928

$\mathcal{I}$n the few short years between the beginning of this chapter and the end of the last one, the face of the globe had been completely changed. Dynasties had fallen, nations had been dismembered and empires had been lost. France, the centre of the motoring world, was mourning the best of her young men, while much of her splendid road system was derelict after the traffic of war. England was not in much better case, though her land had not been a battlefield, and Germany was bankrupt.

Yet the world was avid to get on wheels again. At first, second-hand pre-war cars fetched 2 and 3 times their original purchase price and when Rolls-Royce and Delaunay-Belleville were able to re-start their factories on car production, there was a long queue of *nouveaux riches* with pockets full of folding money, as always happens after a war. However, the Rolls was basically the old Silver Ghost, which was a 1906 design, and the 45/50 hp Delaunay, though a 1914 conception, was still unmistakably an Edwardian.

The young officers, who had fought a highly mechanized war, thought in terms of advanced aircraft engineering. The cars built like railway locomotives by devoted craftsmen did not appeal to them, however beautifully they were made. These men wanted overhead camshafts, light-alloy construction, and 4-wheel brakes, and they wanted them at once.

Many manufacturers felt the same, but their hurriedly designed prototypes were failures. They found that a fuselage construction, which would stand up to the rigours of flying, was unable to resist the incalculable stresses imposed by a bad road. They also discovered that types of engine, which are reliable when maintained by trained aircraft mechanics, soon wilt under the ministrations of chauffeurs and garage fitters.

The man who got it right was Marc Birkigt, and he produced a car that really was a post-war design, yet he kept his feet on the ground. His light-alloy, overhead-camshaft engine of 6½-litre capacity was a smaller version of his aviation power units, but though it was up-to-date, it retained plain bearings and wet sump lubrication, which everybody understood. The chassis was on conventional lines and the transmission included a most basic 3-speed gearbox, which received some criticism. However, Gabriel Voisin's first post-war car was a failure, because its 'advanced' transmission was too clever by half, so Birkigt had reason, as the French say.

Above all, the buyers of powerful cars were crying out for really effective 4-wheel brakes. Manufacturers provided large, ribbed drums and aluminium shoes carrying linings of generous area, but all the cams, bearings, clevis pins, and universal joints, in the mechanical linkage from the pedal, caused much undesirable friction. It took all the driver's strength to operate the brakes when these moving parts were new and well oiled. When the friction had been doubled by grit, mud, and rust, a typical 4-wheel braking system could be less effective than a simple, 2-wheel arrangement.

Most manufacturers tried to overcome the problem by adopting self-wrapping shoes, which were supposed to apply themselves

PREVIOUS PAGES An 8-litre short-chassis Hispano-Suiza sports 2-seater, here being driven at Montlhèry by 'Jabby' Crombac.

The front wheel brakes of the
1919 Hispano-Suiza had
Perrot-type operation by
universally-jointed shafts.

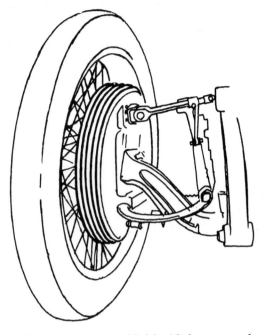

more strongly when the driver had initiated the process by his own feeble efforts. The inventor was Henri Perrot, but Vincent Bendix simplified and cheapened the design by using cable operation. Though this system was developed over a number of years and vast quantities of such brakes were made, particularly by the Bendix Corporation, there were serious flaws. The whole operation was so much affected by the condition of the linings and their temperature, that dangerous locking of the wheels could occur and the adjustment was excessively critical. Many of these self-servo brakes were totally ineffective when going backwards, which could be devilishly awkward! (These remarks do not apply to modern brakes.)

Once again, Birkigt was right, for he applied the necessary assistance close to the driver's foot, and completely under his control. A so-called servo-motor was driven by a worm gear in the gearbox, so that it was always turning when the wheels were moving. It consisted of a small, 2-shoe brake inside a drum, which was applied by the pedal when the driver put on the 4-wheel brakes. Instead of being solidly mounted, the back-plate of this brake could turn, and this it did when the shoes were expanded and tried to go round with the drum. However, the back-plate was coupled to the main braking linkage, so that the torque of the servo-motor was added to the driver's effort in applying the brakes. The braking of the Hispano-Suiza was a revelation and the system was later to be used under licence by Rolls-Royce, among others. To adapt front-wheel brakes to an existing car was never easy, however, and Birkigt had the advantage of designing his chassis for them at the outset.

Externally, the Hispano-Suiza was a big car, with similar dimensions to the post-war Silver Ghost, which had itself grown more bulky with the years. The Hispano had a smaller engine of 100 × 140 mm (6,597 cc), but it developed 134 bhp in its earliest, low-

An 8-litre Hispano-Suiza with a very beautiful open sports-touring body with rear screen.

The light-alloy 6-cylinder overhead-camshaft engine of the Hispano-Suiza was made in 6½-litre and 8-litre sizes.

compression form, so it was considerably faster than the British car. In 1923, a larger version of the light-alloy 6-cylinder engine became available, with dimensions of 110 × 140 mm (7,982 cc).

A short chassis for sporting bodies could be had with either engine size, reducing the wheelbase by a foot, and these cars were very successful in races, the 8-litre version beating Grand Prix cars on occasion and reaching a speed around 125 mph. I have driven an 8-litre 'Boulogne' Hispano belonging to my friend 'Jabby' Crombac, which is almost incredibly fast for its age, attaining 110 mph on any short straight. The chassis is orthodox, with semi-elliptic springs front and rear, but it handles beautifully on corners, although tyre wear is heavy if it is driven hard continuously, owing to its weight.

The more normal Hispano-Suizas, with luxurious coachbuilt bodies, were fitted with lower-geared axles to give flexibility rather than ultimate speed. Marc Birkigt insisted that one should move off in first or second gear and then engage top within a couple of car's lengths. Such driving suited those who still preferred a top-gear car and second gear was, in any case, too low a gear for really sporting handling. The car was not as quiet as a Silver Ghost, the overhead-camshaft, with its vertical driveshaft and bevel gears, being distinctly audible. On the open road, though, it was a wonderfully effortless machine, covering the kilometres in safety at an average speed which one would not attempt in a Rolls or a Delaunay.

At the time of its introduction, the big Hispano-Suiza was incomparably the finest car in the world. It would be superseded, later on, by cars of much simpler construction, that went just as fast and made less noise in doing so. In its day, it was not only the best but also the most beautiful, which is essential for an upper-crust car. That superb radiator, surmounted by the stork mascot of heroic Georges Guynemer's *Escadrille des Cigognes*, reminded the beholder that the flying ace had won his immortal fame with Hispano-Suiza aero engines. The long bonnet suggested the power to go but – a new thing – the big brake drums with their cooling fins emphasized the power to stop.

Though it was designed by a Swiss for a firm of Spanish origin, it was built in their Paris factory and is generally regarded as a French car. Perhaps it was the last time that France, the cradle of motoring and arbiter of taste and fashion for so long, would make a car that could be acknowledged as the finest of them all. In its own country, it completely annihilated The Car Magnificent, the Delaunay-Belleville thereafter becoming just another medium-sized car. Both Delage and, briefly, Hotchkiss tried to share the Hispano-Suiza market, but the snob-appeal of a double-barrelled name, and the association with France's war hero, were too much.

In England, Rolls-Royce ran into an unexpected trouble. After unloading the first batch of post-war Ghosts, they found that marked sales resistance had developed. Several new competitors had sprung up and were undeservedly successful, simply because too many of the wrong people had become Rolls owners. It is regrettable that those contemptible fellows, the war profiteers, invariably bought

Rolls-Royces, and so people who really wanted a Rolls had a Lanchester or a Daimler instead, just to be different from those cads. It seems incredible now, but immediately after the first world war it was 'not quite the thing' to own a Rolls-Royce.

Something had to be done pretty quickly and it was decided to reverse the company's policy, of many years standing, to make only one model. A 20 hp car was introduced to supplement the big 40/50 and it saved the day. The Twenty, followed by the 20/25 and the 25/30, was to provide the firm's bread and butter, right up to the second world war. The various 40/50 hp models continued to maintain the prestige of the great name, but more than twice as many of the smaller cars were sold.

The Twenty was a dull car with little performance but it was beautifully made, totally reliable, and lasted for ever. Many of us bought them secondhand because they gave cheaper motoring than popular makes that wore out quickly. The small Rolls-Royce was not really an upper-crust car, but it was more suitable for an owner-driver than the bigger models, which made it a practical proposition as fewer families kept chauffeurs.

The Hispano-Suiza had servo-assisted, 4-wheel brakes in 1920, but the front wheels of the Silver Ghost were brakeless until 1924. When the Rolls-Royce brakes appeared, they resembled those of the Hispano in many respects and were truly excellent. They never seemed to need relining and those big, heavy cars could really stop. However, they added a good deal to the chassis weight as did the electric starter and 4-speed gearbox, while the bodies seemed to get larger and heavier every year. There was only one thing to do, which was to gear the car much lower; and when I had a 1911 Ghost and a 1924 model simultaneously, the respective weights were 36 cwt and over 50 cwt, while the axle ratios were 2·7 and 3·7 to 1. Obviously, the older car had an incomparably more lively and effortless performance, in spite of the aluminium pistons of the younger vehicle.

In 1925 Rolls-Royce at last dropped the Silver Ghost and introduced the New Phantom. It was, in effect, a Ghost chassis with a new overhead-valve engine. This was an orthodox unit, with pushrod-operated valves and a single carburettor, of 7,668 cc. It gave a welcome improvement to the performance of the big limousines but its high chassis did not permit the coachbuilders to follow the fashion for lower rooflines. The New Phantom, in spite of its engine and its brakes, was still an Edwardian in too many respects. As we shall see later, it was merely a stop-gap while something better was being prepared.

In the early post-war era, many cars were designed to occupy the throne of The Best Car in the World. In passing, it seems odd that so much money and effort were spent to capture what must have been quite a small market, but no matter. Among the British contenders, 2 rivals appeared immediately after the war with 6-cylinder, over-head-camshaft engines having identical cylinder dimensions of 101·6 × 127 mm (6,178 cc). This is not so surprising as it seems, for it represents a bore and stroke of exactly 4 × 5 ins.

The Rolls-Royce New Phantom, which was really a new overhead-valve engine in the existing Silver Ghost chassis. This one carries a *cabriolet de ville* body by Hooper.

The cars were the 40/50 Napier and the 40 hp Lanchester, which differed greatly from each other in spite of sharing the same engine size. Napier had concentrated on very powerful aero-engines during the war and the 40/50 marked their return to the automobile sphere. Like the Hispano-Suiza, it had a light-alloy engine of advanced design, though with a detachable cylinder head, while the name of Napier was great on land and in the air.

Yet the new Napier simply did not sell, perhaps because S. F. Edge had 'had words' with Montague Napier in 1912. Conceivably all that the car lacked was the dynamic showmanship of that extraordinary man. It did not have the silence of the Silver Ghost, but then nothing else had; it was also slower than that veteran car though, which scarcely justified the considerable complexity of its engine. It was certainly produced for too long without front-wheel brakes and by the time they were available, the company seems to have lost heart.

The Lanchester was entirely different. It had its cylinders in 2 detachable cast-iron blocks, which avoided many of the problems that could assail Hispano and Napier owners. Though it was normal to have non-detachable cylinder heads on the more powerful cars, the Lanchester had only its exhaust valves seating directly therein, the inlet valves, which needed less cooling, being in detachable cages. It was thus possible to replace an exhaust valve through the hole left by removing an inlet cage, which was an important sales feature. Rolls-Royce chauffeurs were accustomed to decarbonize one cylinder at a time, so that the car could be made available for use in a few minutes if necessary. The Lanchester design put the overhead-camshaft engine almost on an equality with a side-valve that had individual valve caps.

Even by modern standards, the head design was excellent and though the standard car had its speed deliberately restricted by the use of a single carburettor, twin-carburettor Lanchesters took many long-distance records and proved capable of well over 100 mph in racing trim. The engine and gearbox were mounted in unit in the modern fashion, but the transmission was epicyclic, though with a normal right-hand gearlever and gate change. Once again, there was a curious reluctance to fit front-wheel brakes, though the smaller 21 hp Lanchester had them, but when they did appear it was seen that George Lanchester had invented a new kind of hydraulic servo, operated by the oil pressure of the gearbox lubrication pump, plus an accumulator.

The Forty was exceptionally well sprung and its appearance was attractive, with a delightful little window on the radiator header tank to show the level of the water. It was probably a better car than the Ghost or the Phantom except in one respect, but that was the cause of its downfall. The overhead-camshaft was driven by a vertical shaft through skew gears, and further gears drove a lay-shaft, parallel with the crankshaft, along the left side of the engine. From this shaft, 2 pairs of skew gears were connected to the vertically mounted dynamo and starter motor, the latter through a free-wheel device, while further skew gears drove a cross-shaft for the magneto and water pump from the vertical shaft.

These gears were quiet enough at a steady speed, but they chattered unforgivably when the engine was idling. Right at the end of its production, the Forty was redesigned to have fewer gear drives, but by then the company was in poor financial straits and it was perhaps too late. Nevertheless, this great car was owned by almost as many celebrities as the Daimler, being a particular favourite with Indian Maharajahs, while the Duke of York had 2 of them before he was King, followed by the later 30 hp straight-eight.

Nowadays, most engines will not 'tick over' really slowly; they are comparatively noisy when idling, and we accept it as normal. In earlier days, people judged the quality of a car from the degree of silence attained by its engine when running very slowly in neutral, which they loved to demonstrate to their friends. Though George Lanchester had redesigned his epicyclic gearbox to give quieter idling than that of the pre-war 38 hp model, he then produced an engine which suffered from a proliferation of gear drives. As an engineer, he wanted to make the commutators and brushes of his dynamo and starter, and the contact-breaker and distributor of his magneto, instantly accessible; in achieving this, he flouted the vanity of his customers, replying to their criticisms by suggesting

The 40/50 hp Napier looked rather old-fashioned, in spite of its advanced engine design, and it did not sell.

The light-alloy overhead-camshaft engine of the Napier had a detachable cylinder head, unlike most of the upper-crust cars.

that they should switch off the engine when the car was stationary!

I can never understand how a board of directors can suddenly abandon a major project after sinking large capital sums in it. Yet, that is what the Leyland Company did when they decided not to go ahead with their great 8-cylinder car, but to stick to their excellent lorries only. Their designer, the famous J.G. Parry Thomas, had produced a 7,266 cc straight-eight, in which he overcame the noise problem by driving the overhead camshaft through triple eccentrics and connecting rods. (It should be remembered that chain drives had not reached their present state of perfection and toothed belts were far off in the future.)

The chassis design was as advanced as that of the engine and although rigid axles were still employed, anti-roll torsion bars were used to keep the body on an even keel. The car probably had more performance than anything else then available, though there was little opportunity to use its speed capabilities on the roads of 1920 and maybe some prospective purchasers decided that the machine would be too fast for them. At all events, only a few Leyland Eights were sold and then manufacture ceased. Perhaps the price, which was higher than that of a Rolls or Hispano, put off even wealthy buyers, or more likely the rather ugly radiator shape did not appeal. The car had no front brakes when introduced and perchance the cost of developing these, and of overcoming some teething troubles,

The 40 hp Lanchester carried its overhead-camshaft engine under a conventional bonnet, but retained the crash-proof epicyclic transmission.

The Leyland Eight, designed
by J. G. Parry Thomas, the
famous racing driver, soon
went out of production owing
to a change of policy by its
manufacturers. This open
touring body was the work of
Vanden Plas.

daunted the manufacturers. It's impossible to place the Leyland
Eight among the upper-crust cars of its day, because too few were
made and we do not know how they would have stood up in private
hands. It remains a fascinating enigma, which might have become
one of the greatest cars of all.

W.O. Bentley started building his immortal cars in 1921 but his
'hairy' 4-cylinder sports models are outside the scope of this book.
In 1925, he introduced his big 6-cylinder luxury car, with 4 valves
per cylinder, 12 sparking plugs, but only 1 carburettor. The overhead camshaft was driven by triple eccentrics, like that of the
Leyland Eight, but though the $6\frac{1}{2}$-litre engine was not highly
stressed, it was not as smooth and quiet as some of its rivals. The
gearbox was frankly noisy and needed more skill than many of its
owners could muster, but the springing was the worst feature, being
remarkably uncomfortable on bad roads. The $6\frac{1}{2}$-litre Bentley was
to find its true *métier* when it became the Speed Six, as the next
chapter will show, but it was not sufficiently refined to take on the
leaders of the upper crust.

There remains the position of the Daimler to assess. Though
these chassis often carried magnificent bodies by Hooper, the
royal coachbuilders, they gained the reputation for a somewhat
sluggish performance. This was justified to some extent until 1923,
when new engines were designed with light steel sleeve-valves

instead of the heavy cast-iron ones. It was not so much the weight of the sleeves that mattered as their thickness, the improvement in heat transfer allowing the engines to be tuned for greater speed without the previous danger of seizure.

It is now fashionable to deride the Silent Knight engine because of its heavy oil consumption. It's perfectly true that Daimlers used quite a lot of oil, but so did most of the contemporary poppet-valve cars. Even the Silver Ghost had a consumption that would appear very heavy to modern eyes, partly because, like the Daimler, it had an arrangement for feeding extra oil to the cylinders when the throttle was fairly far open.

The 45 hp Daimler of 7,413 cc was a very large chauffeur-driven carriage of the early post-war years, with infinite dignity but only moderate acceleration. However, when Laurence Pomeroy, Senior, then the Chief Engineer and later Managing Director, designed his flyers, the 35/120 was a really fast car of 5,764 cc, equally suitable for the owner or his chauffeur to drive, while the 25/85 was surprisingly lively. In 1926, Pomeroy mounted 2 25/85 cylinder blocks at 60 degrees on a single crank-case to make a 12-cylinder engine of 7,136 cc. King George V had one of the prototype 12-cylinder engines dropped into his 35/120, which must have been quite a car, but when the 'Double-Six Fifty' was announced, it was seen to be a monster with a wheelbase of 13 ft 7 ins – the short chassis was 12 ft 11½ ins! Daimlers always tended to make their cars too big and this one was really vast, weighing 43½ cwt as a bare chassis without any body. There was also a 'Double-Six Thirty' of 3,744 cc, but the car was so big and heavy that it had to be geared very low and had a pretty dull performance.

If the big 12-cylinder engine had been available in a reasonably light and compact car, the Daimler could have been near the top. Indeed, a couple of low-chassis sports models were built privately but the Daimler directors were not amused. After producing some cars with 3-speed gearboxes integral with the back axle – always a disastrous arrangement – Daimler went back to orthodox 4-speed boxes. Four-wheel brakes became available in 1923 and were greatly improved in 1927 when the Dewandre vacuum-servo was adopted. If I had to describe the Daimlers of this era in a few words, I would say, 'pomp and circumstance on wheels'.

So much for the British upper crust. We have already discussed the Hispano-Suiza and the Delaunay-Belleville but France also had the greatest white elephant of them all. This was the Bugatti Royale, which was supposed to be a car for kings and rulers of states, though in fact none of these exalted beings ever bought one. Indeed, in the 9 years during which the car was catalogued, only 3 firm orders were booked, though 3 more cars were built and used initially by the Bugatti family and for exhibitions.

As befits such a very large car, Ettore Bugatti had a very large accident in one, damaging both himself and his vehicle quite severely. The Royale was exactly like a smaller Bugatti model seen through a magnifying glass, with a straight-eight overhead-

The Daimler Double-Six of 1927 had a 12-cylinder sleeve-valve engine of 7.1-litres and a wheelbase of just under 13 ft. The ultimate in chauffeur-driven luxury, it was patronized by royalty. This limousine body was built by Stratton Instone Ltd.

camshaft engine of 12,763 cc and wheelbase and track measurements of about 15 ft and 5 ft 6 ins respectively. The front axle was on semi-elliptic springs and the rear one, which was combined with the gearbox, on reversed quarter-elliptics. The gearbox gave 3 speeds, top being an overdrive.

This huge car was claimed to be capable of 125 mph, but it was not particularly smooth or silent and was a bit lorry-like to drive. As it cost £6500, compared with £2500 or so for the other upper-crust cars such as the Rolls-Royce, it is not surprising that M. Bugatti failed to get many orders. Luckily for him, he received a substantial contract for Royale engines, which were used with success in railcars.

Ettore Bugatti had delusions of grandeur, but his huge Royale was a white elephant and failed to attract any of the kings and potentates for whom it was designed.

The other French monster was the 40 CV Renault, called the 45 hp in England. This, again, was like a small Renault scaled up, with its radiator at the back of the engine, cooled by air from blades around the periphery of the flywheel. Its side-valve engine was Edwardian in conception, with a bore and stroke of 110 × 160 mm (9,123 cc). The electric starter had a button on one front dumb iron so that you could use the starter and the cranking handle simultaneously, which was ominous!

The standard wheelbase was 12 ft 4 ins, which was not exceptional for a luxury car, but its appearance was immensely impressive, so the President of the Republic used one on state occasions. The 40 CV had the reputation of being difficult or even dangerous to handle at high speeds, but in the short distance I have driven one I merely found it rather heavy and by no means silent, though the brakes, with a gearbox-driven servo, were powerful. Some people thought that the big car was very ugly, but there was one body style known as the skiff, a tiny boat-decked 2-seater, which was as beautiful as it was absurd. The 9-litre Renault was remarkably cheap for its size, a saloon costing £1795 in 1928, but it was rather too crude for an upper-crust car.

The big Renault was very successful in taking long-distance records and so was the straight-eight sleeve-valve Panhard et Levassor. Its 6,355 cc engine gave a lot of power but it was neither smooth nor quiet and was heavy to handle. With a wheelbase of 12 ft 6 ins, it could carry formal 7-seater limousine coachwork. The Farman, a French car built expressly to be the best in the world, had an overhead-camshaft engine of 6·5 litres, later increased to just over 7 litres. It was a huge vehicle and lorry-like in the extreme, while the steering was the heaviest that any car has ever had!

Let us go from France to Belgium, where 'The Goddess of Automobiles' was born. The Minerva was yet another sleeve-valve car of which numerous models were made, with 4, 6 and 8 cylinders. Of these, my favourite was the 32/34 hp 6-cylinder of just under 6-litre capacity. It was one of those marvellous cars that divine providence seems to inspire so very infrequently and the Minerva Company had the good sense to go on making it, alongside much later models, for more than a decade.

The standard chassis had a 12 ft $5\frac{1}{2}$ ins wheelbase and could carry the most elaborate bodies at speeds which could hardly be believed, very powerful servo-assisted brakes making fast motoring safe. There was a short-chassis sports version, too, which was quiet and refined but could get along at over 90 mph. I remember an old gentleman called Mr Baker who used to come to Brooklands in one of these, a magnificent open sports 4-seater with front and rear windscreens. His uniformed chauffeur would remove the lamps and mudguards, whereupon Mr Baker would race and probably win. After the Brooklands meeting was over, the Minerva would tour silently into the Surrey countryside, where the chauffeur would hand round the tea and cakes as the Baker family took their ease. Truly, this was how a gentleman should go motor racing!

The engine of the Bugatti Royale was a straight-eight of 12,760 cc with 3 valves per cylinder, operated by an overhead-camshaft. The cars proved virtually unsaleable but the engines were used, 4 at a time, in high speed French rail-cars.

Louis Renault's huge 40 CV 9-litre, here carrying the President of the French Republic at a state occasion

The Minerva was not an expensive car, except when fitted with particularly elaborate coachwork, but it must rank high in any list of upper-crust vehicles. Personally, I found its slightly bulbous radiator with rounded shoulders attractive and full of character.

Italy had the Isotta-Fraschini, a make which had front-wheel brakes even before the war. Only one model was made, which lasted from one war to the other, a big straight-eight that began at 5,881 cc but was soon enlarged to 7,372 cc. There was a standard chassis and a sports version with a tuned engine, called 'Tipo Spinto', which could also be had with a short wheelbase when it was called 'Super Spinto', one of which I owned.

The Isotta had quite a simple engine with pushrod-operated overhead valves, the cylinder heads (2 in line) and block being of

cast iron. The standard of construction was very high indeed and
one could open the bonnet with pride to show one's friends the
exquisite engine. It was a most elegant vehicle, on which many
delectable bodies were built, but the engine ran surprisingly roughly
for a machine of this calibre and the car was rather hard work to
drive. The gearbox had only 3 speeds but the engine gave so much
torque that this hardly mattered. It was an impressive car that
would last for ever but it fell short of upper-crust standards of
refinement and had a terrifying thirst for petrol.

Italy's other contender was one of those mystery cars. Designed
and produced at great expense, its manufacture was suddenly discontinued after only a very few had been made. The car was the
Super-Fiat, with a 12-cylinder engine of 6,805 cc. The big engine
was extremely neat and tidy, as were all Italian power units at that
time, the valves being operated by pushrods and the gearbox having
3 speeds. The drums of the 4-wheel brakes were enormous and the
rear springs were cantilevers, as were those of the majority of large
cars. It was a car of impressive appearance, with a radiator slightly
reminiscent of a Rolls, and why its manufacture did not continue is
still a well-kept secret.

In Germany, life was hard indeed and Mercédès and Benz were
obliged to combine to keep their heads above water. They produced
some spectacular cars for export, in which a Roots-type supercharger was driven at high speed through gears from the crankshaft;
a clutch engaged when the accelerator was pressed down to its
limit and put the blower in motion. The resulting banshee wail was
an inspiring sound to the enthusiast and all part of the character of
the cars, but unacceptable for the upper crust, I'm afraid. Teutonic
styling seldom appealed, but Mercedes-Benz produced an open

119

Minerva, 'The Goddess of Automobiles': this superb Belgian sleeve-valve car could cover long distances at high average speeds with deceptive ease.

OVERLEAF Weymann fabric-covered bodies, often built under licence by British coachbuilders, were extremely fashionable for a short period. This 6½-litre Bentley has the typical *faux compas* (dummy hood irons) to disguise the blind rear quarters.

sports 4-seater that was low and extremely attractive. However, these cars were not at all refined and their brakes were inadequate for their speed and weight.

After the war, it was again possible to design one's own body and have it built at a reasonable price. Visits to the coachbuilders were still social occasions, as they were when Samuel Pepys had his first horse-drawn coach made and recorded the scene in his diary. Glorious walnut veneers, the finest leather hides, and more than 20 coats of paint, each laid on and then laboriously rubbed down by hand – these were some of the ingredients used in building any high-class body, but the skill of the individual craftsmen was the most important constituent.

Then came a total change in method that seemed likely to revolutionize the coachbuilding industry. This was the Weymann body, in which a light framework was covered with fabric in place of metal panels. In the true Weymann body, the wooden frame members had metal joints, so that no 2 pieces of wood could touch and creak. The fabric was spread over the frame but was sufficiently flexible to let it move about as the chassis frame twisted over bumps. Thus, the prevalent trouble of creaking bodies and split panels was eliminated.

The Weymann body was incredibly light and, by its very nature, it was wonderfully silent and suppressed mechanical sounds instead of magnifying them. The rather angular lines came as a pleasant change after too bulbous shapes, the matt finish of the fabric also giving a businesslike appearance. At the same time, some new styles appeared, notably the sportsman's coupé, a close-coupled body with a very large luggage trunk behind. These bodies often had blind rear quarters, relieved by dummy hood irons resembling those of a drophead coupé.

This chapter ends at 1928, when the Weymann body was at its zenith of popularity, but already there were cheap copies which were to discredit the whole system and make fabric covering totally unacceptable.

It had a short life but it did not deserve to die. Nevertheless, the traditional coachbuilders must have heaved a sigh of relief when the fashion ended as quickly as it had begun.

The post-war recovery was at an end and a world depression was in the offing. Indian Maharajahs, exempt from normal standards of taste, were still displaying their wealth by having their cars decorated with jewels and precious metals. Among less exalted mortals, an opulent appearance was now to be avoided and cars were generally finished in sober colours.

Some firms banned their directors from coming to their factories in makes of car that were known to be very expensive, for fear of upsetting the staff. If you were well off it was bad form to mention it, and vulgar display was a deadly sin; perhaps it would be no bad thing if such reticence were practised nowadays. The Great Depression was looming up and soon almost everybody would be poorer than they had ever imagined possible.

6
The Great Depression
1929-1931

The Rolls-Royce Continental Phantom II was often fitted with flared mudguards of dashing appearance, though they were not very effective at catching the dirt.

When they married and gave in marriage,
  They danced at the County Ball,
And some of them kept a carriage.
  And the flood destroyed them all.

*T*he 1920s started off in a blaze of post-war gaiety. People lived extravagantly, even wildly, and there were parties galore. They rolled back the carpets and they danced to the gramophone, and to the popping of corks. Never mind the mess, for there were plenty of servants to clear up afterwards. It was a wonderful time to be rich.

Then, gradually, something seemed to go wrong. The unemployment figures kept rising and shares did not pay the dividends they should. The money ran out and so did the champagne; the parties ended and nobody felt like winding the gramophones any more. Dance music had been everywhere and this was the sound of the 1920s, but as the decade faltered towards its close, the music stopped and everyone was very sober indeed.

It had been a most exciting period in motoring history; in a few short years, the cars and the scene had changed completely. People drove faster, because the new 4-wheel brakes made it safe to do so, while bigger and better tyres not only reduced the danger of skidding but did not burst if the car was given its head on a long straight road. Speed was no longer a 5-letter word and fast driving under suitable conditions was not considered anti-social.

Perhaps the greatest change had been brought about by the electric starter. It became normal for a lady to drive herself, instead of something rather dashing and courageous. As cars grew more numerous, their reliability also improved and there were plenty of garages waiting to attend to their wants. If a car broke down, even a gentleman might drive past without stopping, which he would never have contemplated previously – the freemasonry of the road was vanishing, alas!

In many countries, the roads were becoming over-crowded, while a curious disease manifested itself in England. This was the practice of building by-pass roads to avoid towns, and then allowing speculative builders to erect miles of ghastly little houses right alongside them. Somehow, the right hand did not seem to know what the left hand was doing, or perhaps a crate of whisky to the county surveyor worked wonders. In France, the *Routes Nationales* were straight enough for sustained speed, if your springs and tyres could stand the bumps and pot-holes, but in most other countries acceleration and braking were the most valuable features.

As always, the road conditions influenced the design of the cars and while the French automobiles, of necessity, had the best suspension, the Italian engineers learned all about brake fade in the Alps and their vehicles could be recognized by their enormous finned drums. Cars that were quite adequate performers in England often proved to be almost useless on the Continent, which was why Rolls-Royce did all their testing in France.

It had been a valuable period in the development of the motor-car, but suddenly the world was plunged into a crisis so violent that many manufacturers were annihilated. In France, there had been some 350 car factories in operation during the 1920s but by 1932, only 23 remained. Some other countries were not quite so hard hit, but even those *marques* which survived had often received mortal wounds.

The depression started spectacularly with a tremendous slump, the Wall Street crash, and millionaires flinging themselves from the tops of the New York skyscrapers, if the popular press was to be believed. By the time it ended, at some indeterminate date 2 or 3 years later, the havoc was even more widespread than that of the Great War itself.

Logically, this should have been a time for smaller and cheaper cars. Yet even modest firms, which had never made powerful cars before, announced new straight-eights instead of baby 8 hp models. Like Gadarene swine, they rushed to their destruction, but even the factories with truly great names brought out larger and more costly cars. Incredibly, into this world of poverty, famine, and 'Buddy, can you spare a dime', were born the Rolls-Royce Phantom II, the 12-cylinder Hispano-Suiza, and the Bentley Speed-Six and 8-litre!

Most of these cars were put on the market almost before they were really ready, and the reason for this unseemly haste is plain. Even those people who were still quite wealthy had stopped spending their money on luxuries in the prevailing gloom, so the firms were unable to find customers for their existing models. Almost their only assets were the experimental vehicles which they had been developing for the future, as every manufacturer does. They were doomed if they could not start selling cars again, so they had nothing to lose. They rushed their prototypes into production and these exciting new models proved irresistible. The strategy worked, even if the customers had to contend with some unexpected teething troubles.

It may seem curious that people were willing to buy these very large cars at a time when money was short. In the distant past, only a big engine could avoid the gear-screaming crawl up hills that was the curse of the low-powered car. By the time of the depression, medium-sized cars could almost equal the performance of the giants. Yet, there was little incentive for big-car owners to try something smaller, because petrol remained surprisingly cheap throughout the depression and car taxes were not increased.

If Rolls-Royce had continued to build the New Phantom, owners would have stuck to their present cars. Instead, they introduced the Phantom II and degraded the existing model by calling it Phantom I. The Phantom II looked so low and modern by comparison that its predecessor became old-fashioned overnight – once a Rolls-Royce chauffeur had seen the new car, he would start discreetly nagging the guv'nor until a chassis was placed on order.

The Phantom II chassis was a coachbuilder's dream. There were no cantilever springs to get in the way of the rear doors and a hypoid-bevel back axle lowered the propeller-shaft line, permitting the floor level to be dropped. Previously, coachbuilders had preferred to work on Daimlers and Lanchesters, because of their underslung worm-drive rear axles, for a flat floor was essential in the rear compartment of an upper-crust car, where folding occasional seats were usually fitted.

Nothing remained of the Silver Ghost in the Phantom II chassis, which was really a greatly enlarged version of the 20 hp car. The engine and gearbox were mounted in unit and the torque tube was deleted in favour of an open propeller shaft. The torque reaction of the rear axle was absorbed by the flat semi-elliptic springs, on the principle known as Hotchkiss-drive. Naturally, the superb brakes, with their gearbox-driven servo, were retained and it is worth noting that they were just as effective as the best modern disc systems but lasted far longer without requiring any attention.

The engine was a development of the Phantom I unit, with 2 cast-iron 3-cylinder blocks united by a single light-alloy head. The dimensions were 108 × 139·5 mm (7,668 cc), the compression ratio was 4·75 to 1, later raised to 5 to 1 and then 5·25 to 1, while the valves were operated by pushrods and rockers. There were 4 different gearboxes during the 6 years of the model's currency, all delightful to handle with the right-hand gate-change, which was still preferred for upper-crust cars. At first, the box was plain, but then synchromesh appeared on third and top and was finally used on second gear as well.

I owned a 1929 Phantom II, which I used as my everyday car for a considerable period, as well as doing some long-distance touring. The appearance was magnificent, for the Barker *sedanca de ville* body had been built to the order of the Hon Dorothy Paget. Incidentally, the Hon Dorothy also had a very beautiful open touring body on one of these chassis, which I have seen her drive in a most terrifying manner while her chauffeur, on the back seat, indicated by not so much as a twitch of the eyebrows that he was undergoing the tortures of the damned. Truly, a Rolls-trained chauffeur was the aristocrat of his very exacting profession! The Phantom II was a big car with a 12½ mpg thirst, but it held the road splendidly and handled like a small sports machine.

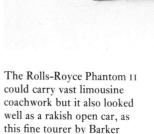

The Rolls-Royce Phantom II could carry vast limousine coachwork but it also looked well as a rakish open car, as this fine tourer by Barker proves.

However, if the chassis was outstanding, the engine was a bit of a disaster. It had immense low-speed torque and the car would climb almost any hill on top gear, while the acceleration was surprising for so heavy a vehicle. Yet the engine was remarkably rough and at a cruising speed of 70 mph it was pretty noisy, too; the Rolls-Royce testers christened this model 'gutty-rough', not without reason. The Phantom II was a charming car to drive but it could not approach the Silver Ghost for silence and smoothness. One feels that it was introduced before it was really ready and later versions of the engine, with a much stiffer crankshaft and an improved torsional vibration damper, were not so coarse.

The Phantom II carried some beautiful bodies by the best coachbuilders, both formal 7-seaters and, on the Continental chassis,

close-coupled coupés; perhaps no other car has ever looked quite so elegant. It was beautifully made, with that multiplicity of tiny studs and bolts holding everything together, that was so typical of Rolls-Royce engineering. It was also outstanding value for money when the chassis price was reduced to £1750, £100 less than the last Silver Ghost.

Though many Rolls-Royces were still chauffeur-driven, the Phantom II was the first 40/50 that could easily be maintained by the owner. The later chassis even had a 1-shot lubrication system to look after the innumerable lubrication points, which is something of a contrast to my 1911 Silver Ghost; it has about 100 greasing and oiling places, spread all over its anatomy. The instruction book tells me how many minutes I should allow my man for each job, the maintenance tasks taking 1 hour and 53 minutes at the end of every week, plus a few chores which occupy 5 hours and 17 minutes (if wood wheels) or 5 hours and 57 minutes (if wire wheels) each month.

That I always take far longer than these times merely proves that I have not been trained in the Rolls-Royce school for chauffeurs.

Perhaps it also underlines that the Phantom II had certain advantages over the Silver Ghost after all.

Rolls-Royce had hit upon the right formula in producing 2 models and when the New Phantom was replaced by the Phantom II, the Twenty gave way to the 20/25. This 3,699 cc car had only a modest performance, though it was up-rated quite considerably during its lifetime, but while the total Phantom II sales were 1,767, those of the smaller car were more than double that figure. Although the Phantom II, with all its dignity and glamour, was the flagship, the 20/25 had no teething troubles and must have proved a little goldmine.

RIGHT The long, low look of the Rolls-Royce Phantom II suddenly made earlier models seem old-fashioned.
BELOW A typical interior of a limousine on a Phantom II chassis, showing the low, flat floor permitted by the hypoid axle.
BELOW RIGHT The 20/25 hp Rolls-Royce, here seen with a Weymann close-coupled 'sportsman's coupé' body, was small enough for ladies to drive without fatigue and its economy was appreciated during the Great Depression.

The overhead-camshaft Hispano-Suizas were no longer at the top of the market. The complicated, light-alloy engines could have their problems when no longer new, and garages found them difficult to service. Accordingly, the makers brought out 2 new models with pushrod-operated valves, an immense 12-cylinder of 9,424 cc and the 4,900 cc K6, which used many parts from the bigger car, and followed a little later.

The 12-cylinder Hispano-Suiza was another of those cars which was just too big and failed to capture the public imagination. The chassis cost £1000 more than the Phantom II and the yearly tax in England, under the absurd 'horsepower' formula, was £75 compared with £44 for the big Rolls-Royce. Its worst feature was the 3-speed gearbox, which purchasers were no longer willing to accept in a quality car. The gear ratios were very oddly chosen, too, first gear being so high that the clutch was apt to suffer when starting away against a steep gradient.

This gearbox, when used on the 6-cylinder car, was simply ridiculous, and I failed to climb the Butte de Montmartre one night when baulked by crawling traffic, having to reverse down to a more level stretch before taking off again! The 12-cylinder was a well-proportioned car, but somehow the coachbuilders were never able to give it the lightness and grace of the earlier Hispanos; it certainly looked a bit stolid compared with a Phantom II.

Nevertheless, the *douze-cylindres* was capable of a very genuine 100 mph when fitted with luxurious bodywork. It suffered, like all the other cars of its era, from lack of development, but the money was simply not available in those grim days. It was a vicious circle, because the demand was insufficient to justify the costly modifications which were desirable, yet without these improvements there could be no increase in sales.

There were those Frenchmen who insisted that the 12-cylinder Hispano-Suiza could have found more customers if it had won the 24-hour race at Le Mans. Whether or not the car was suitable for such an exercise, it is difficult to say. The fact remains that the make which won Le Mans repeatedly, and many other long-distance races, too, failed to survive the great depression.

In the early 1920s, the 3-litre Bentley was the car which every red-blooded young man longed to own. It was a practical sports car with many exciting features that came straight from racing, but its 5-year guarantee made it seem like a safe investment. Above all, it was the right size, and its long-stroke engine was taxed at only £16.

If W. O. Bentley had stayed in that class, he might have weathered the storm. Instead, he attempted to take the upper-crust market away from Rolls-Royce which, with his small firm and inadequate finances, was courageous but hardly wise. The 6½-litre Bentley had an inferior chassis to the Phantom II but its overhead-camshaft engine, with 4 valves per cylinder, was capable of far more development than the 'gutty-rough' power unit of its rival.

In single-carburettor form, the big Bentley engine was nothing out of the ordinary, but with twin SU instruments as used in the

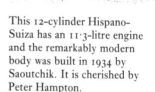

This 12-cylinder Hispano-Suiza has an 11·3-litre engine and the remarkably modern body was built in 1934 by Saoutchik. It is cherished by Peter Hampton.

Speed-Six, it was marvellously smooth, very powerful, and has never been excelled for high-speed reliability. As developed for Le Mans by Harry Weslake, it could maintain a power output in the 200 bhp bracket.

Much of the financial backing of Bentley Motors came from Captain Woolf Barnato, a multi-millionaire who was also one of the best racing drivers of his day. It was his driving, as much as his money, that made the name of Bentley great, but it was probably his preference for big cars that brought about the final downfall. The great Speed-Sixes, painted in British racing green, were a wonderful sight as they took the lead in race after race. With light competition bodywork, they seemed to handle quite well, but in normal, road-going form they frightened quite a few of the customers.

Probably the chassis frame was insufficiently rigid, among other things, but the Speed-Six could be quite a handful when fitted with closed coachwork. It was not well sprung and its gearbox was both noisy and difficult to manage, but it was a good-looking car with a great name. W.O. Bentley was aware of its deficiencies, but he had a new and even bigger car on the stocks.

The chassis of the Speed-Six Bentley, showing the 6½-litre overhead-camshaft engine and the right-hand gate change, which was a 'must' for upper-crust cars.

OPPOSITE W. O. Bentley is the passenger in this open Speed-Six with body by Vanden Plas.

A Speed-Six Bentley in Le Mans trim, driven by Woolf Barnato with Sir Henry (Tim) Birkin as passenger.

The cylinder dimensions of the Speed-Six Bentley were the same as those of the overhead-camshaft H6 and H6B Hispano-Suizas and when W.O.Bentley wanted to make his 8-litre, he again followed Birkigt's measurements as used in the H6C, 110 × 140 mm (7,982 cc). Very wisely, he retained the 4-valves per cylinder and silent, eccentric-driven overhead camshaft of his 6½-litre engine. The chassis was altogether more modern, being extremely rigid and with the rear springs outrigged as closely as possible to the wheels.

Unfortunately, the prevailing fashion was followed in having an excessively tall radiator, with bright metal shutters in front of the core as in a Rolls-Royce. The roadholding was the best of any Bentley yet, but the first batch of engines were far from satisfactory, much thicker castings having to be adopted – a most unwelcome expense at that time. There was no money for a proper development programme, but the 8-litre went magnificently nevertheless. It was the first saloon car in which I ever travelled at 100 mph and the acceleration seemed breathtaking in those days.

Properly developed, the 8-litre Bentley would have been a better car than the Phantom II, but more money was needed. A synchromesh gearbox would have been necessary, for instance, which would have been very costly to design and get into production. With potentially the best car in the world on his hands, W.O. Bentley ran out of cash and 'Babe' Barnato turned off the tap. To the utter disbelief of the entire motoring world, the Bentley car was allowed to die.

Friction-type shock absorber and Perrot brake on a Bentley.

This 8-litre Bentley, the property of Peter Agg, has been restored to as-new condition. A December 1930 *Autocar* road test gives the 8-litre saloon a timed maximum speed of 101·12 mph.

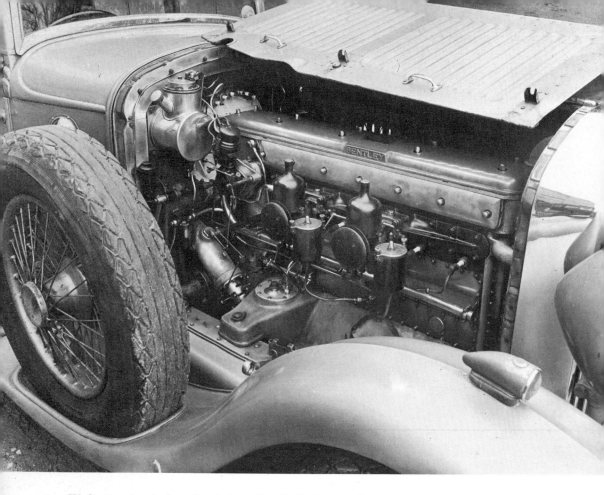

W.O. Bentley had realized that, like Rolls-Royce, Lanchester, and others, he must produce a medium-sized car, for the upper-crust market alone could not provide a living. Accordingly, he instituted design studies for an entirely new, 6-cylinder, 4-litre engine. Impressed by the success of American side-valve engines, he did a lot of work on a single-cylinder test rig of that type, but for some reason he abandoned this configuration for an inlet-over-exhaust arrangement.

This engine was notably lacking in torque, which was made more noticeable by the excessive weight of the complete car. The chassis was virtually an 8-litre with shorter side-members, which resulted in a ponderous vehicle compared with the sprightly little 20/25 Rolls-Royce. The 20/25 was often driven by the daughter of the house, but the 4-litre was really too clumsy for her use. The dear old 4-cylinder 4½-litre Bentley had been an exhilarating car to drive with its Vanden Plas open body, but when closed bodies were required, even for sports cars, it was intolerably noisy, though perhaps it had been bearable with a Weymann fabric saloon.

So, the superb 8-litre had no effective running mate and the cost of a rescue operation would have included the production, from scratch, of a new medium-sized car. Tears are still being shed about the Bentley tragedy, but the firm had reached the end of the road.

The engine of the 8-litre Bentley was a logical development of the Speed-Six, with four valves and two sparking plugs per cylinder.

Even the 8-litre would shortly have needed replacement by something with more and smaller pistons. The great sixes of over a litre per cylinder had passed their apogee; one would never again open a louvred and riveted bonnet with the same flourish as if one were inviting privileged guests to walk round the engine room of one's yacht.

During the period under review, the big 6-cylinder Mercedes-Benz, designed by Dr Porsche, were nearing the end of their production. With overhead-camshaft engines and screaming superchargers engaged at the driver's will, they had increased steadily in size from the K of 6·25 litres in 1926, to the low-chassis s and ss of 6·8 and 7·1 litres. Extremely impressive, even arrogant cars, with their V radiators and huge plated exhaust pipes emerging from the side of the bonnet, they were really too noisy to be acceptable with closed coachwork. They were heavy to drive and splendid for developing the muscles of the right leg when braking, but the performance was not as good as that of a Speed-Six or 8-litre Bentley, in spite of the supercharger, though the 'works' competition cars were considerably faster.

Yet I must write of one of the great cars of all time, for there was a short-chassis version, called SSK, of which a very few lightened ones, SSKL, had an oversize supercharger and other modifications. These cars had an immense performance and were raced with great success, particularly by Rudolf Carraciola. As the ultimate manifestation of the vintage-type blood and thunder (or *Donner und Blitzen*) sports car, the SSKL will be for ever remembered, though it is rather outside the scope of this book.

Like so many other firms, Mercedes-Benz produced a monster in 1930, again with a supercharged overhead-camshaft engine but this time a straight-eight of 95 × 135 mm (7,655 cc). It was offered in England at a price around £4000 but there were no takers; indeed it was probably intended as a prestige car for embassies and the like. I have driven most of the cars described in this book but I have never even seen a 'Super' or 'Grösser' Mercedes, while my only photographs are spoilt by a silly little man with a toothbrush moustache, standing up in the back in a 'please, teacher' attitude.

During the production of the big overhead-camshaft cars, Mercedes-Benz also made some more utilitarian models with side-valve engines. None of these concern us except the Nürburg, a straight-eight of 4·6, later 4·9 litres. Sad to relate, it had a remarkably lethargic performance, but one of the few which came to England was modified by L.C. McKenzie, the Bentley wizard, who made two holes in the cylinder block communicating with the induction passages cored therein. Attaching a pair of carburettors, he presented the delighted owner with a car that went as no Nürburg had ever gone before. This model was extremely well made but it was out-performed by American straight-eights at a fraction of its price.

In England, we were singularly ignorant for many years of the best American cars, though the cheaper models were always admired for their toughness and lack of needless frills. During the 1920s and 1930s, American cars became more and more popular, in spite of the adverse effect of the 'horsepower' tax on their big-bore engines. A wealthy friend of mine made the mistake of buying a Duesenberg, a huge car which was full of sound and fury, signifying nothing. However, the Stutz was greatly admired, having a straight-eight overhead-camshaft engine of 4,811 cc, later increased to 5,277 cc. The Stutz was one of the few American cars to have a Weymann fabric body and it gave the Bentleys a run for their money at Le Mans.

The American engineers soon mastered the many problems of the straight-eight engine and their simple, side-valve power units greatly influenced European thought. In France, many new side-valve engines replaced overhead-valve types, with combustion chambers copied from American models. Even Lorraine-Dietrich, a firm with a racing history going back to the beginning of the century, produced a 4-litre side-valve luxury car with hydraulic brakes, before sliding into oblivion.

Though there had been British and Continental cars from time to time with hydraulic brakes, it was the Americans who made them a commercial proposition. Similarly, there had been British cars since the start of motoring with easy-change gearboxes but the Americans made such transmissions a part of everyday driving and suddenly a car with a 'crash box' was unsaleable.

Technically, the most important development of the period occurred when Laurence Pomeroy, of Daimler, mated a Föttinger fluid coupling with a Wilson gearbox; it was the Genesis of nearly all the automatic transmissions that are used today, though at that time the gears were pre-selected with a lever on a small quadrant, the actual changes taking place when the left pedal was momentarily depressed and released.

It is quite a fascinating story. Major Walter Wilson, known affectionately as 'Dammut' – his favourite mild expletive – by his mechanics and as 'Tanky' by others, was famous because he invented the military tank. He built the Wilson-Pilcher car in the early days of motoring and among his many inventions was the preselective gearbox. This was not just another epicyclic box, for it had 4 speeds instead of the 2 or 3 that most of these transmissions gave. In addition, the preselective feature was a great advantage, particularly in racing where the Wilson box was extremely successful later on – I raced an ERA that had one.

However, the commercial production was delayed for several years by a most unfortunate circumstance. Major Wilson sold his box to Vauxhall, who had actually built it into several cars when they found themselves in financial difficulties. Although I was only a schoolboy, I was taken for a ride in a 14/40 Vauxhall by Major Wilson at that time, and I was most impressed with the results he obtained with his preselective transmission. I had the luck to live near his home and I quickly realized that he was an engineering genius – an often misused word that really was apt in his case.

The financial difficulties of Vauxhall allowed General Motors to take over and as they were just introducing their new synchromesh easy-change system, they simply sat on the Wilson box so that nobody else could use it. Wilson fought tooth and nail to get his invention back and eventually he succeeded, though quite how I have never discovered. At that time, Daimler were experimenting with a fluid coupling, largely so that the royal cars could travel at walking pace in processions. However, the sliding-pinion gear-boxes that they were using did not work well with the new drive.

The Wilson preselective gearbox was exactly what was required and very soon all Daimlers were fitted with what the company called the Daimler transmission. The preselective gearbox was also chosen for Armstrong Siddeley cars, but in this case the fluid fly-wheel was not employed, which entailed using the first gear band as a clutch when starting from rest. It performed this duty adequately but not particularly smoothly, a criticism which also applied to many other makes, which subsequently appeared with the preselective box. The fluid flywheel, as Daimler called the Föttinger fluid coupling, eliminated the only weakness of the Wilson epicyclic transmission.

This coupling was patented by the Herr Doktor in 1906, was adapted to the automobile by H. Sinclair just 20 years later, and after development by the Daimler engineers it went into production in 1930. It consisted of an outer member, attached to the engine flywheel, and an inner member connected to the transmission. Both members were arranged, in effect, one behind the other, though the driving side also carried a casing which embraced the driven part and was provided with an oil-tight gland, through which the shaft to the gearbox passed.

This casing was kept almost full of oil and the driving and driven members each had a machined surface, these 2 flat faces being set with a small clearance between them. Both members had cup-shaped depressions between vanes cast in their faces, communicating with labyrinthine passageways. At engine speeds below 600 rpm, the oil circulated lazily to and fro between the 2 members and round the ducts, but as the flywheel turned faster, the liquid was propelled with considerable energy from vane to vane and power began to be transmitted to the shaft. As the speed increased still further, the oil, under the action of centrifugal force, became effectively frozen and the whole assembly revolved as one solid lump.

It will be appreciated that a Daimler could be started off in any gear and driven at a snail's pace, but the lower gears were used normally for maximum acceleration. Under extreme conditions, such as starting away on an extremely steep hill with the car fully laden, the gearchange pedal could be used like a clutch to allow the engine to reach high revolutions before engagement. Under all normal circumstances, however, the fluid flywheel gave a smooth and reasonably rapid getaway, the left foot only moving at the moment of gearchanging.

The Daimler transmission formed the basis of subsequent American designs. Instead of manual preselection, however, the Wilson gearbox was controlled by automatic devices that were sensitive to speed and throttle position. Much later, the fluid fly-wheel became a torque converter by the addition of a reaction member, its increased range allowing the epicyclic box to be simplified by deleting one ratio. It is amusing that the Wilson gearbox was superseding the synchromesh box, in spite of General Motors' early efforts to suppress it!

The introduction of the Daimler transmission coincided with yet another re-think on the double sleeve-valve engine. Laurence Pomeroy was greatly enamoured of light alloys and the new Daimler power units employed these materials wherever possible, including even the cylinder blocks. Greatly increased revolutions were possible, to which end the miniature crankshafts operating the sleeves were counterbalanced, while the outer sleeves were lightly coated inside with white metal, to avoid seizure with the inner sleeves.

Two entirely new V12 cars were announced, the 40/50 (6,511 cc) and the 30/40 (5,296 cc), with long, low chassis to carry luxurious coachwork. To encourage the British motor industry in the dark days of 1931, and perhaps to indicate that the depression was almost over, King George V ordered 5 new Double-Six Daimlers, 2 40/50s and a 30/40 for himself, plus a 40/50 and a 30/40 for Her Majesty. Hoopers were commanded to build the most sumptuous bodies, for which they used traditional coachbuilding methods with no modern short cuts; of course, all the interior fittings were either of silver or ivory and there was much polished mahogany.

This has been a sad chapter to write, especially as the circumstances of the depression appear to be repeating themselves, though we have so often been assured that such a thing could never happen. A few pages back, the reader no doubt shed a tear for the demise of the old Bentley Company. Perhaps even more tragic was the announcement, in 1931, that Daimler had acquired the assets of the Lanchester Motor Company.

There were to be new cars called Lanchesters, but they were really Daimlers with Lanchester radiator shells. However, the principal reason for the take-over was the need for technical know-how. Daimler wanted to build cars with 8 cylinders in line, for the straight-eight fashion was approaching its peak. Lanchesters had a superb straight-eight, and as the pitfalls in designing such engines were numerous, they wanted to avoid costly mistakes. Much more radical was their desire to abandon the sleeve-valve engine, for the buying public could no longer be convinced that its formidable complexity was justified. The great car that the Lanchester brothers had conceived in 1895 was no more, but all those years of advanced engineering were not extinguished, for there was more than a breath of Lanchester in the long line of poppet-valve, straight-eight Daimlers that were to come.

The other chapters of this book are named after the outstanding cars of each period of motoring history. This one concerns a dark season when world conditions were all against the production of a masterpiece. Great cars were born, but none of them were without flaws. It would hardly be fair to choose any of them as the supreme example of its age, and so no particular make is commemorated in the chapter heading.

7
Packard
1932-1939

The Great Depression didn't just stop. Recovery was to take years, and in some respects the old standards, which had even endured the war, were to be lost for ever. In all countries, people had been living on a reduced scale and had grown accustomed to accepting second best. Regrettably, craftsmanship and quality were less valued than in the past.

In England, Rolls-Royce and Daimler were the only upper-crust motor manufacturers to survive. Whether or not the Phantom II ever paid for itself, I am scarcely qualified to say; with its relatively small production and the many changes in specification, I would hazard a guess that it did not. The company earned its bread and butter from the 20/25, which later had its cylinder bore increased and was re-named the 25/30.

The emphasis on the smaller car was partly brought about by a great reduction in the number of chauffeurs. They were still used for company cars and by business executives, but there were far fewer in private service. In the past, Rolls-Royce owners had kept a chauffeur, even when they did much of the driving themselves, because of all the chassis lubrication and maintenance tasks. When this work was so reduced that an infrequent visit to the service department sufficed, there was no necessity to keep a man to do the chores.

Perhaps even more important was the revolution in car finishes that took place towards the end of the 1920s. If it were raining when one came home at night, a Silver Ghost had to be sponged down and leathered off or the varnish would be spotted by the morning. Similarly, the copious use of polished brass or nickel-plated fittings meant hours of work with rags and 'Brasso'. To drive a Silver Ghost with a tarnished radiator and dull, stained lamps and accessories would be unthinkable.

When even the best coachbuilders used cellulose spraying instead of paint and varnish, and stainless radiators and chromium-plated lamps ended the tyranny of the polishing rag, a car could be kept quite smart with only an occasional wash. As the general adoption of labour-saving devices, such as electric lighting and central heating, had reduced the size of indoor staffs, so the chauffeur, who had once put the coachman out of work, was now himself redundant.

All this was symptomatic of a great social change, for even in the big houses life was becoming less formal. Families had religiously dressed for dinner during the war, even when there was not much to eat and Zeppelin raids were expected; it was regarded as a duty to keep a civilized home going for the men when they came home on leave from the mud and squalor of the trenches – 'Keep the Home Fires Burning' was one of the most popular war songs. During the depression, there was no such incentive and people tended to live simpler lives with less dependence on servants.

The smaller Rolls-Royce fitted into this new life-style perfectly. It was sufficiently compact to be easy to park but it could carry spacious coachwork, with occasional seats for theatre parties or race meetings, if required. It was often bought by the sort of man who

PREVIOUS PAGES The Packard Eight of 1936 with the makers' standard saloon coachwork.

150

would formerly have run the 40/50 hp model as a matter of course. Consequently, there tended to be an emphasis on the heavier body styles, which rendered the greater torque of the 4,257 cc, 25/30 hp engine desirable. The car was thus moving right away from the light 'sports-saloon' which was often fitted to the 20/25 chassis around 1930, but something much better was to replace it in this field.

When Bentley Motors went into liquidation, the directors of Napier made a bid for the firm. Though they had been totally committed to aero-engine manufacture since 1925, the idea of returning to the automobile world had always attracted them and they considered that a car called the 8-litre Napier-Bentley would surely be irresistible. With the benefit of hindsight, I wonder.

The 8-litre Bentley was an unforgettable car, which I have driven with enormous pleasure. Its few faults could have been eliminated and it would, no doubt, have been a magnificent machine. Nevertheless, the day of the vast 6-cylinder car was over. Of all the legion of big sixes, only the Phantom II remained and its multi-cylinder successor was already in the pipeline. Furthermore, as we saw in the last chapter, a new medium-sized car would also have been needed, for the 4-litre Bentley was a total flop. If Napier had had enough money to start from scratch and let W.O. Bentley loose on the drawing board, they would have stood some chance of success, but merely to continue the manufacture of the 8-litre alone would almost certainly have been a very costly mistake.

In fact, such reflections are completely irrelevant, because when Napier thought that the deal was concluded, a last-minute bid from Rolls-Royce secured Bentley Motors, lock, stock and barrel. The factory and machinery were sold off in due course and few of the personnel were absorbed, but W.O. Bentley was retained, though he was employed more as a tester than as a designer of the new Bentley car. He was justifiably bitter about his subordinate role, but it had been a smart stroke of business to acquire a great name and eliminate a possible rival simultaneously.

Very wisely, the Rolls-Royce engineers forgot all about 'Babe' Barnato's high-speed monsters. The time was out of joint for forays to Le Mans and when 'The Silent Sports Car' made its appearance, it was seen to be a logical successor to W.O.'s first car, the 3-litre Bentley. Like that immortal machine, the new $3\frac{1}{2}$-litre Bentley was the right size. It had all the performance, and more, of its illustrious ancestor, but it demanded none of the skill and physical toughness that the 3-litre had exacted from its driver, nor did it encourage the use of ear plugs when equipped with a saloon body.

The ingredients of the $3\frac{1}{2}$-litre Bentley already existed, as the chassis was the prototype for the 18 hp Rolls-Royce, a more compact version of the 20/25 which was never marketed, because there proved to be no significant saving in purchase price compared with the larger car. This smaller chassis was fitted with an up-rated 20/25 engine, which had a high-compression cross-flow cylinder head and twin SU carburettors.

The gearbox, with a right-hand gate-change, had especially close ratios, the Rolls-Royce servo brakes were naturally used, and flat semi-elliptic springs were employed all round. At a price of £1460 for a saloon, this 90 mph silent sports car was more popular with the customers than any previous Bentley had been. If this was a smaller car than the upper-crust vehicles described in previous chapters, perhaps its inclusion can be forgiven, because it appeared at a time when even the very wealthy were thinking in terms of less costly transport.

Notwithstanding the success of these smaller models, a new 40/50 was needed to replace the Phantom II as the best car in the world. It was time for the last of the big 6-cylinder cars to retire, for though it was still incomparably beautiful, it was becoming technically dated. It had to be admitted that most American cars, with their independent front suspension, gave a far smoother ride than the Rolls-Royce, and – oh horror – their multi-cylinder engines were quieter and vibrated less.

The Rolls-Royce answer was the Phantom III. It was expected that the car would be a straight-eight, with an even longer bonnet than the Phantom II, since that was the fashionable number of

The Bentley as built by Rolls-Royce – 'The Silent Sports Car' – was popular because it was compact and easy to drive. The untidy Christmas tree effect of lamp, horns, mirrors and spare wheels was typical of the 1930s, and the fashionably shallow screen necessitated the bobble on the left wing to show the driver where the other side was.

cylinders at the time and the firm did possess such a power unit. However, their experience with 12-cylinder aero-engines, notably the victorious R-type of Schneider Trophy fame, no doubt influenced the designers and the engine of the Phantom III turned out to be a V12. With dimensions of 82·5 × 114 mm (7,340 cc), the power unit was considerably shorter than the big six; furthermore, the independent front suspension allowed the weight to be carried further forward. Consequently, although the Phantom III had a shorter wheelbase than the Phantom II, a much larger proportion of the chassis was available for coachwork.

With its forward-mounted radiator and shorter bonnet, the new car lacked the elegance of its predecessor. The coachbuilders were influenced by some rather ugly fashions in the middle 1930s, of which more anon, and it was rare indeed to see a Phantom III with the heart-stopping beauty of a Phantom II. A long bonnet and a radiator mounted well back are by no means essential to a graceful automobile, but the master coachbuilders certainly knew how to make the best use of these proportions, while a forward-mounted radiator at first foxed them completely.

To drive, the Phantom III was an incomparably better car than its predecessor. The engine was very smooth and quiet but the power was certainly there and the great car was really fast. Rather surprisingly, the makers reverted to a separate gearbox on this model, with quite a long clutch shaft. This brought the right-hand lever well back alongside the driver's seat, an ideal position which left the door unobstructed. The gearchange was delightful and third was close enough to top to be useful for overtaking at quite high speeds. In 1938, a gearbox incorporating an overdrive top gear was fitted, as it was to the Bentley, in 1939.

The independent front suspension, made under General Motors patents, was of the wishbone type and gave an excellent ride, while the steering was quite light, though this was before the days of power assistance. I never owned a Phantom III myself, but a friend had one who preferred drinking to driving. I sometimes volunteered to chauffeur him, just for the pleasure of handling his car and I often saw well over 90 mph on the speedometer. The body of this particular Phantom III was low-built and comparatively light – one would not expect this sort of performance from a limousine, of course, and I was glad that I was not paying for the petrol.

It is fairly well known that the Phantom III was not without teething troubles, notably in the camshaft area, which is curious as worn cams were not unheard of in the Phantom II. The cars were hastily modified and the hydraulic tappets deleted, but once again it would seem that a bit more testing would not have come amiss. Perhaps the test drivers and maintenance engineers were too kind to the cars, or was there a rush to hit the deadline to introduce the new model? Incidentally, it is the practice of some French manufacturers to fit their prototype engines to the cars of selected farmers and commercial travellers, who can be relied upon to expose

any weakness far more rapidly than the most ruthless professional tester!

Having tackled the teething troubles of the Phantom III, the Rolls-Royce engineers set about modernizing the 25/30. A new chassis was designed, with independent front suspension and a wheelbase longer by 4 ins which, coupled with the further forward mounting of the engine, gave a vastly increased space for the body. The Wraith was a town carriage *par excellence* but rather dull on the open road. Just before the war, the $4\frac{1}{4}$-litre Bentley engine and overdrive gearbox were dropped into a new chassis with inde-

ABOVE The Phantom III as a drophead coupé. The high radiator and waistline gave a poor view from the interior but were greatly admired in the 1930s.
BELOW A 1936 12-cylinder Rolls-Royce Phantom III sports saloon. The shallow windows and the waistline drooping towards the tail were fashionable.

pendent front suspension, designated Mark V. Only a few were built before hostilities put an end to fine car construction.

During this period, Daimler had the painful duty of replacing the sleeve-valve engine, to which they had been faithful for more than 20 years. Their task was made easier by the immediate popularity of the fluid flywheel and preselective gearbox. The new poppet-valve engines appeared first in the smaller models and though it was tricky to explain the reasons for the change to the public, the cars gained ready acceptance.

Unfortunately, Pomeroy's all-aluminium sleeve-valve engines had done nothing to enhance the renown of the name, so the relatively new Double-Sixes were quietly phased out. They were replaced by a straight-eight with poppet-valves, which subsequently became two distinct types, a $4\frac{1}{2}$-litre chassis for the formal coachwork beloved of traditional Daimler customers, and the 'Light Straight-Eight' for owner-drivers, which was aimed at the Bentley market. The engine was of about the same capacity as the $3\frac{1}{2}$-litre and when the Bentley went up to $4\frac{1}{4}$ litres the Daimler was hurriedly bored out to 4 litres. The $3\frac{1}{2}$-litre cost £1050 and the 4-litre £1070 with saloon bodies, which seems impossibly cheap for such quality. It was an outstandingly good-looking car, untouched by the ugly fashions of its period, but at first it was out-accelerated by its rival. However, the Bentley gained a lot of weight when its rather whippy frame was replaced by a heavier one, the two makes then being more on an equality.

The crunch came when King George V ordered a new Double-Six, to be completed for the spring of 1935, which was to be just as high as the previous state limousines but considerably wider. He had been a great enthusiast for sleeve-valve engines all his life, but Daimler hoped that he would not insist on this type of power unit. However, it was whispered that the aluminium engines had been giving some trouble on the royal journeys; at all events, the monarch was talked into his first poppet-valve car. It had a nice, simple $6\frac{1}{2}$-litre V12 engine, with cast-iron detachable heads and cylinder blocks, and rumour has it that similar units were quietly insinuated

The Daimler fluid flywheel, here seen partly dismantled, suited the Wilson preselective gearbox admirably. It was ideal for royal processions at walking pace.

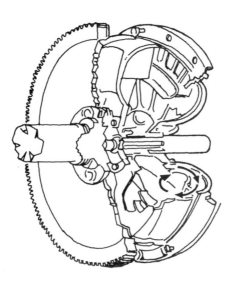

into the existing royal cars. These 6½-litre Double-Sixes were never catalogued.

Subsequently, the production 4½-litre straight-eight was ordered as a royal car by King Edward VIII during his brief reign, though he used a Buick on his unofficial trips and had run first Crossleys and then Rolls-Royces while Prince of Wales. King George VI also had straight-eight Daimlers, some of them fitted with Lanchester radiators as a tribute to the make he had always driven; he was the best driver in the Royal Family and preferred to handle his small sporting Daimler drophead coupé himself. At his coronation, I watched the cars taking the peers and VIPs to the Abbey and about 90 per cent of them seemed to be Daimlers, some of splendid antiquity with equally venerable occupants. Though the market for chauffeur-driven cars was diminishing, the Daimler Motor Company certainly had the lion's share of it at that time.

Although the straight-eight models had simple engines with pushrod-operated valves, they had one design feature that made it almost essential to take them to Daimler Service at Hendon for an ordinary valve-grinding and decarbonizing job. Their heads and cylinder blocks were cast integrally, which had theoretical advantages and eliminated the gasket, but the task of lifting the block and, more particularly, of later inserting eight pistons in the bores without breaking any rings, was usually beyond local garage ''erberts'. The much smaller Lanchester Roadrider was similarly constructed, which infuriated keen amateur mechanics.

Rather surprisingly, a third contender for the super-car market emerged in England. In the 1920s, the Lagonda was a very small car with one of the first combined body and chassis constructions. Then a 2-litre sports car appeared, followed by a 3-litre, a 3½-litre, and a 4½-litre 6-cylinder with the well-known Meadows engine, which was later to win the 24-hour race at Le Mans. Incredibly, this steady growth had gone on right through the depression and, in 1935, a very disgruntled W.O. Bentley walked out of the Rolls-Royce factory and travelled to Staines, where Lagondas were made. His brief, believe it or not, was to design a 12-cylinder car.

The V12 4½-litre Lagonda was a most ambitious project. With a single chain-driven overhead camshaft per bank, the engine was installed in a rigid chassis with independent front suspension, which was unfortunately very heavy. It was sold in 3 lengths, the longest for limousines, prices starting at £1550 for a short-chassis saloon.

On fast roads, the big Lagonda would travel at speeds close to its maximum indefinitely, putting up extraordinary averages for that era. This characteristic was emphasized when 2 almost standard chassis, with remarkably little preparation, came third and fourth in the 1939 Le Mans. Yet, the car was unpleasant to drive at lower speeds, being excessively heavy to handle, with a noisy engine and gearbox, while the lack of torque necessitated too much gearchanging. Reluctantly, we must drop the Lagonda from our upper-crust team.

The 12-cylinder Lagonda, designed by W.O. Bentley, was capable of sustained high speeds but was rather noisy and heavy to drive. This is a 1939 short-chassis Rapide.

There were other British contenders, notably Alvis, who built a 4·3-litre luxury car. It was most disappointing to drive and the independent front suspension had some unpleasant habits. Sunbeams, who had made many excellent medium-sized cars in the past, commissioned Georges Roesch, of Talbot fame, to design a new straight-eight. Unfortunately, it suffered from the dreaded torsional vibration of the crankshaft and a re-design was judged to be too expensive by the new proprietors, the Rootes brothers.

In France, the big Hispano-Suiza proved too big and costly and few were sold. A larger engine of 11,310 cc became available, which had been developed for rail-car use, but the demand for 11-litre cars was minimal. Ettore Bugatti continued to build cars of outstanding individuality, but none of them offered the riding comfort and quiet running that one expects of an upper-crust car. Louis Renault had a huge side-valve straight-eight of over 7-litre capacity called the Reinastella, but it was the sort of thing that the Americans were doing so much better. There was a rather rare short-chassis Reinasport with a very long bonnet, with which actresses were wont to win *concours d'élégance*, but I was told by my French friends that it was an accident waiting to happen.

There remains the Delage, of which I can speak with experience. Louis Delage built a 4-litre straight-eight which was always a good-looker, especially when the very low sports chassis with an immensely long bonnet appeared. I had one of these, with a dramatic drophead-coupé body by Fernandez et Darrin, which was not as fast as it looked but reasonably rapid nevertheless. M. Delage was always short of money and so his straight-eight was obliged to make do with the same gearbox and brakes as his smaller cars. I twice stripped the first and second speed pinions and I was always relining the brakes, but it was such a pretty car!

Neither this nor the 4·3-litre straight-eight that succeeded it were really upper-crust cars. The best Delages were the smaller 6-cylinder models that were closely related to Delahayes. There was a D6-70 in my family for many years, with that lovely Cotal electric gearchange, which ran for years with complete reliability.

In Italy, that incredible anachronism, the Isotta-Fraschini, was still selling to America, because it looked so beautiful. It is curious that Lancia, with independent front suspension, had been showing us, since just after the first world war, that the rigid front axle should be superseded. Yet, it was not until American cars began appearing with 'knee-action' that everybody rushed into the design of independent front ends. Though the Lancia chassis were worthy of inclusion in any list of upper-crust cars, even the 8-cylinder engines lacked refinement when judged by the highest standards.

In Germany, Mercedes-Benz had discontinued the tough, blood-and-thunder sports cars, replacing them with the 540K, which was less sporting and had independent suspension of all 4 wheels. A straight-eight of 5·4 litres, it had the usual voluntarily-engaged supercharger, but it was of enormously heavy construction and rather disappointing to drive. It seemed curious that a firm which was making ultra-light and immensely powerful racing cars did not let some of that technique rub off on the production cars. The traditional 7·7-litre straight-eight was awarded a completely new chassis with independent suspension, but though this model continued to be catalogued, it seemed to be largely reserved for top Nazis.

There was, at this time, some technical liaison between Mercedes-Benz and General Motors in America, which was known to exist in engineering circles but received no publicity. The front suspension of the larger General Motors cars was modelled closely on that of the Grand Prix Mercedes-Benz racing cars, as can be seen at a glance. The smaller General Motors cars, such as Chevrolet, Vauxhall, and Opel, had the Dubonnet system, for which royalties were paid to the French inventor. Though the majority of technical advances were not American in origin, the American engineers had an incomparable genius when it came to putting them into production. The manufacturing techniques used in Europe were years out of date by comparison, for there was still an almost religious devotion to hand work and a reluctance to admit that there were things which a machine could do better.

The great American corporations became masters of the principle, long adopted by Rolls-Royce on a smaller scale, of letting the sales of popular models pay for the production of the prestige cars at the top of the range. Costly research into metallurgy and casting techniques, for example, could be financed by vast mass-production enterprises but was far beyond the reach of the specialist manufacturer, even of the most expensive cars. The Chevrolet and the Buick made the Cadillac possible and the humble Ford subsidized the lordly Lincoln. Above all, the popular '120' Packards must be respected because it was thanks to them that, for a few short but wonderful years, the incomparable Super Eights and Twelves could be sold at highly realistic prices.

Cars can be judged as mechanical works of art or regarded as rich men's playthings; nevertheless, the best car in the world must be the one that is the most reliable over an immense mileage. An upper-crust car may be the better for skilled maintenance, but it must continue to give excellent service when neglected or spared the most perfunctory attention. It must be able to stand being driven flat-out for hour after hour or day after day and must never be sick or sorry. Such cars were the Silver Ghost and the Delaunay-Belleville, but most emphatically, the Phantoms and Hispano-Suizas of the 1930s were not of this calibre.

The Packard brothers started building automobiles in 1899 and by 1904 their product was a shaft-driven 4-cylinder car of useful performance. The Packard car grew up in the tough days of American motoring but by 1911 a luxurious 6-cylinder model was catalogued, described by an executive of the Packard Motor Car Company as 'a car built by gentlemen for gentlemen'. In 1915 the first v12, called 'Twin-Six', appeared, but it was no hothouse plant. When the USA entered the war, the top brass rode in Twin-Six open touring cars to the front. All the filth, over-loading, and neglect that war service entails could not daunt them, and they gave such magnificent service as did the Rolls-Royce Silver Ghost armoured cars. General Pershing's Twin-Six, still in khaki paint, takes part in French rallies nowadays.

In 1923, a straight-eight with front wheel brakes, called the 'Single-Eight', replaced the Twin-Six at the top of the range and a new 12-cylinder model was not announced until 1931. For more than a decade after that, the straight-eight and v12 were manufactured side by side, the former satisfying the majority of customers, for it could hardly have been more silent and the acceleration was brilliant.

The Packard Super Eight and Twelve of the 1930s – the names Single-Eight and Twin-Six were soon dropped for the Senior range – were of very similar design. Their engines had side-valves and detachable cylinder heads but, whereas the Super Eights had orthodox vertical valves, those of the Twelves were considerably inclined; they were operated from a single central camshaft by roller-bearing rockers, with automatic adjustment of their fulcrum positions by hydraulic pistons. There was some variation in the

A gorgeous 12-cylinder Packard of 7·7-litres, the open touring body having a rear screen and concealed hood; it was built by Murray. One of these cars was delivered to the White House.

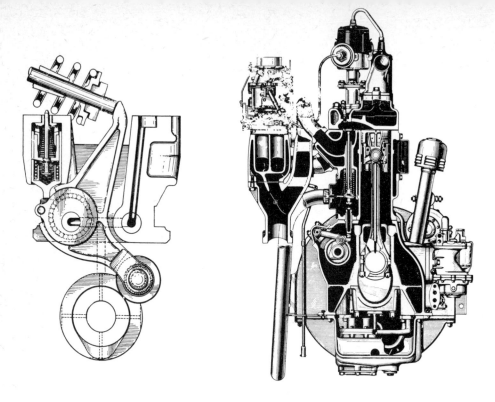

size of the eights during the period under review, but the principal types were of 5·3 and 6·3 litres, giving up to 150 bhp. The 12-cylinder engine was soon increased from 7·3 to 7·7 litres and was developing 202 bhp in 1935. Aluminium crank-cases and detachable cast-iron cylinder blocks were used and aluminium heads replaced the cast-iron ones early in the 1930s.

Though a 4-speed gearbox was fitted for a while, American drivers, unlike their British cousins, preferred a 3-speed synchromesh box. The single dry plate Long clutch had a vacuum servo to give light pedal operation on the Twelve, the vacuum servo for the brakes having a 4-position dashboard control on all Senior models. This allowed the servo assistance to be reduced on icy roads or increased for women drivers. The very large Bendix brakes were cable operated, to be replaced by Lockheed hydraulic brakes at the time that independent front suspension was adopted in 1937, rather later than by the other American manufacturers and after 2 years' experience on the low-priced 120 and 110. Prior to that, semi-elliptic springs with front shackles had been used, with a kick-shackle to prevent shimmy. Deep channel-section frames were employed, with a hefty X-bracing amidships, and the front end was also boxed and braced on later cars. In the early and middle 1920s, a very typical Packard feature had been the steel disc wheels, mounted the 'wrong' way round with the cone pointing inwards. Wire wheels then became the normal wear, with pressed rims on the Super Eights and rolled ones on the Twelves, followed by orthodox discs; the hub caps, of whatever type, invariably had a central hexagonal depression that was like a trademark. A low propshaft line was achieved in 1926 by adopting the hypoid axle.

ABOVE LEFT The self-adjusting rockers operated inclined side-valves in the Packard Twelve engine. ABOVE Cross-section of the Packard Super Eight engine, with detachable cylinder block and aluminium crank-case. Note the accessible location of the double distributor.

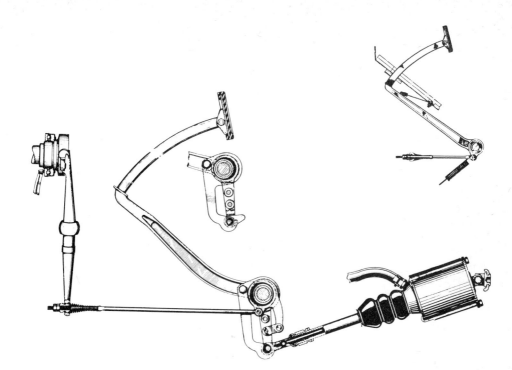

It would have disgusted the experts of 1920, who were crying out
for advanced light-alloy overhead-camshaft power units, to realize
that the homely, iron-block Packard engines were lighter and much
more powerful, size for size, than the beautiful Hispano-Suiza
power units of aero-engine design. The immense progress in side-
valve technique was largely founded on the pioneer work of Sir
Harry Ricardo in England, but the Americans took it from there.
By clever design of the cylinder heads to give controlled turbulence,
it was possible to obtain an excellent power output with smoother
and quieter running than comparable overhead-valve units could
provide. These advantages have now been nullified by the universal
adoption of over-square dimensions, for it is impossible to obtain
an acceptably high compression ratio in a side-valve engine when
the stroke is very short.

The lubrication system included a heat-exchanger in the water
circuit, which gave rapid warm-up and efficient oil-cooling thereafter. This was no doubt an advantage with the Twelve but scarcely
necessary with the straight-eights, of which the very long sump
gave a huge cooling area, a great advantage over the v8 configuration.
Other precautions to ensure long engine life included duplex fan
belts, while reliable ignition was guaranteed by twin coils on the
Super Eight, operated by a 4-lobe cam and twin breakers, the
distributor cover having 2 tracks corresponding with a pair of
brushes in the rotor. The Twelve naturally had twin coils.

Exaggerated importance is often attached to performance figures
and they have little to do with the more desirable attributes of an
upper-crust car. Packard never made speed claims and nor did
Rolls-Royce, but it is perhaps permissible to glance at some

ABOVE The 12-cylinder Packard engine with inclined side-valves, which develops 202 bhp.

RIGHT J.C.Denne's beautiful Dietrich-designed *sedanca de ville* by Le Baron, on a 7·7-litre 12-cylinder Packard chassis, shows how little the radiator shape has changed over the years.

contemporary road tests. The smaller 5·3-litre straight-eight Packard, costing £895 in England, ran rings round the Phantom II, both for speed and acceleration, but was beaten by the Phantom III, by 1·8 mph in maximum speed and 1·9 seconds for 0–60 mph acceleration. The Twelve usually carried very elaborate coachwork but when less heavily encumbered it was capable of well over 100 mph, though silence and smoothness were its most outstanding characteristics.

It used to be customary to criticize early American cars for their low-geared steering and soft suspension. This was largely because most of the cars we drove then had extremely hard springing and heavy steering, but if one drives an early Packard nowadays, the handling is remarkably similar to that of a modern car; the steering is not so low-geared as that of other contemporary American makes. In the opinion of J.C.Denne, the well-known Packard expert and collector, the cars continued to improve until 1934, after which a gradual cheapening process began, at first almost imperceptibly.

The complete separation of popular and Senior Packards was no longer practised and such things as the twin fan belts and double distributor were later omitted from the Super Eight. Styling changes detracted from the patrician elegance and the Packard began to look more like the other American cars, which it had never before resembled. The bigger straight-eight was dropped in 1937

A Packard Super Eight chassis being overhauled by J. C. Denne, which is to be fitted with a roadster body.

164

and by 1939, the 5·3-litre Super Eight used the chassis and body of the popular 120, with a big bulge in the firewall to accommodate the longer 9-bearing engine. Even a steering-column gearchange came with this package and the magic had gone. The one 'real' Packard left was the Twelve and only 446 were made in 1939.

This sad change had been unavoidable, for in 1938 the Senior models had been only 8 per cent of the total Packard production but had occupied 50 per cent of the labour force. The year 1937 was the best ever, with a total of 109,518 cars, but the figure for the following year had fallen to 49,163, so rationalization was essential and it was impossible to go on making Seniors regardless of time and money. Nevertheless, over the period from 1932–39 the Packard was the best car that money could buy – remarkably little money, too. As the makers' slogan said, 'Ask the man who owns one', and let us not forget that in the coming war, Rolls-Royce were to choose Packard to build the Merlin aero-engine.

In Europe, and particularly England, it was an all-time low for automobile engineering, largely because of the brain-drain to the aircraft industry, and some unbelievably bad cars were made. In bodybuilding, the fashions were completely decadent and bogus. Impractically low rooflines were used with long and ridiculously high bonnets, necessitating a windscreen so shallow that it was like the slot in a letter box. A high waistline and a reduced window area contributed to the driver's poor all-round view and to the funereal darkness of the body interior. To add to the false impression of a long engine, the hinged bonnet was carried right back from the radiator shell until it almost reached the windscreen, the scuttle penetrating under the rear half of it. Often, there was less bonnet length containing the pathetic little engine than the bit that covered the legs and feet of the occupants, who had the windscreen almost touching their noses, while the steering wheel massaged the driver's stomach.

Worse still, from a structural point of view, were those huge doors that hung down below the chassis. When the body sat upon the side members of the chassis frame, it was comparatively rigid and the cutouts for the doors were of reasonable size. The heavy doors usually caused their hinges to drop in a very short time, but as they formed the larger part of the body sides, there was no rigidity in the structure at all. When the doors were opened, the sham was revealed, for the low build was all an illusion and one had to step up over the relatively high chassis members. Such bodies were often built very heavily, in an attempt to obtain some strength, but when they were light they broke up fairly rapidly and the worst ones have mercifully not survived.

Having ruined the body, the stylists turned their attention to the wings and running boards. A proper running board is made of wood, which acts as an expendable protection against side impact and can be cheaply and quickly replaced. A gentleman's car also needs running boards, so that his friends have somewhere flat to stand their glasses when spectating at sporting events. The stylists

The 2/3 seater roadster, with a 'rumble' seat in the tail, was one of America's most popular body styles. This is a Packard Eight coupé-roadster of 1934.

A Rollston Allweather Cabriolet, which could be mounted on either the Packard Super Eight or the Twelve chassis.

were evidently teetotallers, for they threw away the running boards, and the wings, too, replacing those with little mudguards more suitable for a bicycle.

This fashion did not appeal for long, simply because the cars became so plastered in mud that even the windscreen and windows were covered and the door handles were too dirty to touch. It was then realized that the running boards were necessary, but they were not reinstated. Instead, the front wings were continued in a sweeping curve until they met the front of the back ones. Where one was supposed to tread, the paint was protected by little strips of metal with rubber inserts, which worked as long as a high-heeled shoe did not score the polished surface in between. The mud was kept down all right but these pseudo-running boards gave poor crash protection and were expensive to replace. Above all, they were entirely useless for their main purpose of supporting glasses.

The great coachbuilders were entirely innocent of encouraging these decadent fashions, though they could not entirely ignore them. No other profession demanded such craftsmanship and integrity as this, the apprenticeship being long, strict, and arduous. Yet, most of the bodybuilding firms of repute were in financial difficulties at this stage, for the bodies on many cut-price cars were not even made by genuine coachbuilders. They were built as cheaply as possible by newcomers to the business, who lacked the necessary experience and training and who used inferior materials and unseasoned timber. Superficially attractive, these bodies were bound to give trouble later on, when they were found to be almost impossible to repair. Among the cognoscenti, these flashy vehicles were usually described as 'cads' cars'.

Meanwhile, the demand for special bodies of the highest quality was lower than ever before. Customers were impatient and bought cars off-the-peg, thus missing the exquisite pleasure of watching bodies that reflected their own personality as they grew day by day to unhurried perfection. It has been said that the combined pressed-steel body and chassis killed the specialist coachbuilders, but their world was coming to an end many years before that. The mass-production car was delivered ready for the road and buyers of expensive models no longer had the leisure or inclination to equip them to their own ideas. A tradition that went back to horse-drawn carriages was coming to an end.

As for the coachbuilders, some of the best were absorbed by the motor manufacturers, notably in the USA and in England. Several British firms went over to Spitfires and Hurricanes instead of luxury cars, for a frenzied rearmament programme was in full swing, but most of the smaller workshops just faded away.

It may seem curious that there was such a craving for make-believe cars, which looked faster and more expensive than they were. With the depression just behind them and the dictators beating the war drums, people felt desperately insecure. Nothing seemed permanent and, when they dared to think about it, a war seemed inevitable sooner or later, which would probably bring about the end of civilization. Half unconsciously, they were trying to compress as much living as they could into the time that was left, so it's hardly surprising that they were attracted by the tinsel show rather than solid worth; they bought new cars for excitement and who cared how long they lasted!

8
Camargue

The Rolls-Royce Camargue, designed by Pininfarina and built by Mulliner Park Ward, brings Italian aggressiveness to a make that usually relies on British understatement.

*M*odern warfare is all tragedy and suffering, for the glory departed long ago, if it ever really existed. Following the second world war, the devastation was far worse and more widespread than after the first. British factories had been bombed by the Germans and German factories had been completely flattened by the British and the Americans; French factories had been thoroughly plastered at different times by both sides. The Italians, though deeply involved in the conflict, during which they had changed their allegiance, apparently managed to go on building racing cars – but nothing could stop them from doing that!

The Americans were in a far better position for their factories had been remote from the war theatres. In the USA, the stoppage of car production had been for a comparatively brief period and it was to be expected that they would consolidate their pre-war leadership with little difficulty. Instead, they built huge, impractical cars with none of the toughness which the British had always admired in the past. They were of startling appearance, with voluptuous curves, high tail fins, and huge, chromium-plated dragons' mouths. Never has an opportunity been so wantonly thrown away.

These cars wallowed on their soft suspension – the advertisements spoke of 'boulevard ride' – and on wet roads they were quite terrifying to drive. They failed to live up to the former go-anywhere reputation of American cars and their brakes were almost useless. This was peculiar, because some of the earlier USA productions were noted for their fine brakes, but the new models were so much faster and heavier while illogically their brake drums were smaller.

All this was particularly sad, because the new overhead-valve American v8 engines were truly excellent. When used in European chassis, such as Bristol, Facel Vega, and Jensen, they set very high standards for performance, flexibility and smoothness. They lacked the sump area of the previous straight-eights, however, and it was best to use an oil radiator for sustained speed.

The great name of Packard was applied to an exciting new v8-engined car, with torsion bar suspension inter-connected front and rear, which automatically levelled the car electrically according to load. My mother ordered one of these, which I subsequently inherited, and I timed it by stopwatch at 109·7 mph. Its smoothness and silence were unequalled at that time, but the brakes were dangerously inadequate, which new British linings failed to cure. No doubt the American roads were straighter than those of Britain, while their speed limits discouraged 100 mph motoring, but it was no good having all that performance and not being able to use it, so the Packard had to go.

Just before the war, there was an experimental Daimler with 2-pedal control – in other words, the fluid flywheel and Wilson gearbox were converted to automatic operation, as described in chapter 6. The American engineers seized on this idea and though the first automatic transmissions were called 'jerk-o-matic' by the unbelievers, improvement was rapid. As usual, it took American enterprise to commercialize a British invention and they were soon exporting their excellent transmissions across the Atlantic.

England had taken a pounding in the war and it was some time before car manufacture could be restarted. Rolls-Royce decided that the Phantom III would be too complicated and expensive to make and to maintain under post-war conditions and let it slip into history, without too much regret, perhaps. Many of the traditional engineering features had to be abandoned, such as the vast numbers of tiny bolts that held mating surfaces together and the bolted and riveted construction of the chassis. Driving gears for the dynamo and water pump were replaced by a belt, as on other cars, and saddest of all, the centre-locking wire wheels were superseded by bolt-on discs. It was almost impossible to obtain high-quality materials and body panels tended to have a wavy surface that would never have been tolerated in the old days.

The first post-war car was developed from the smaller Rolls-Royce, the Wraith, which in its turn had descended directly from the 25/30, the 20/25 and the Twenty. It was an orthodox steel x-braced chassis which the few remaining coachbuilders could clothe with their bodies, with wishbone-type independent front suspension and semi-elliptic rear springs. The post-war Bentley, the Mark VI, had a similar frame with a shorter wheelbase and, for the first time ever, a steel body made by the company could be specified.

An entirely new engine was used, though many of its dimensions were still those of the pre-war $4\frac{1}{4}$-litre unit – it was subsequently to be bored out to 4·5 and then 4·9-litre capacity. The cylinder block and crank case were machined from a single iron casting, with the exhaust valve seats in the side-valve position; the inlet valves were in the head. The inlet-over-exhaust arrangement had all the advantages of a side-valve design in achieving controlled turbulence of the mixture, but it gave a more compact combustion chamber.

Engines for Rolls-Royces had one carburettor and those for Bentleys had 2, except that the last Silver Wraiths had power units to Bentley specification. There was also a sort of cocktail, the Silver Dawn Rolls-Royce, which was the shorter Bentley chassis with the Rolls-Royce radiator and a single carburettor; it often carried the standard steel body, too. From about the middle of 1952 to 1955, a greatly improved version of the Mark VI chassis was called the R-Type.

The R-Type Continental was an unforgettable car. With a comparatively small and light coupé body and a highly tuned engine, it had a high-geared back axle and a gearbox with astonishingly close ratios. It was a joy to drive and wonderfully effortless on a long journey. Its only disadvantage was the difficulty of engaging the unsynchronized bottom gear when changing down from the extremely high second. The R-Type Bentley was the first Rolls-Royce model to be offered with an optional automatic transmission, by courtesy of General Motors.

In addition to their cars, the company made power units for various purposes and a range of petrol engines was available with

the inlet valves over the exhausts, with 4, 6, and 8 cylinders. A specially refined version of the six was used in the cars and the original intention was to install the big straight-eight in a larger vehicle to continue the Phantom series. The straight-eight 5,675 cc Phantom IV was a heavy chassis for 7-seater limousines, with a 12 ft 1 in wheelbase. It was never offered to the public and only 16 were made to special order between 1950 and 1956, for royalty and heads of state.

Various lighter cars were fitted experimentally with straight-eight engines, but it was found extremely difficult to make the front end rigid enough. Independent suspension needs a frame that does not flex or twist and whereas the old straight-eights, like the Bugatti and the Isotta-Fraschini, relied on their solidly mounted engines to brace the forward part of the chassis, modern engines float on rubber and cannot be used for this purpose. Consequently, a long engine means that the side members lack cross-bracing where they most need it. Like the Americans, the Rolls-Royce engineers decided to abandon the straight-eight for this one reason.

The Continental Bentley was a silent, high speed car that seemed a veritable magic carpet in the early 1950s.

Though Rolls-Royce are now of integral construction, a few frankly old-fashioned chassis are still made for the state limousines and landaulettes that were once a Daimler monopoly. This is a Phantom VI by Mulliner Park Ward.

The Silver Shadow brought integral construction and independent self-levelling rear suspension to 'the Best Car in the World'.

Though I have no blue blood in my veins, I have driven the big straight-eight. In my case, however, it was not propelling a Phantom IV but a Dennis fire engine, which it did at commendable velocity. Rolls-Royce continued to use the 6-cylinder power unit in their new Silver Cloud model, but it was later replaced by a light-alloy V8 of 6,230 cc, in which a reversion to pushrod-operated overhead valves took place. The Silver Cloud was the last model with a separate chassis frame on which coachbuilt bodies could be mounted, but most of them were fitted with the standard steel body – the equivalent Bentley no longer differed in anything but radiator shape.

Since the war, mass-production cars had assumed a new shape, with wider bodies that usurped the functions of the wings and running boards. The more conservative customers found the new cars unattractive at first, applying the epithet 'slab-sided'. Though all-enveloping bodies were more vulnerable in traffic, the obvious gain of interior space won the day, while reduced wind resistance promised more speed. These lower, wider bodies were difficult to build on separate chassis frames, so integral construction finally invaded the upper-crust market.

Perhaps the Silver Cloud was rather too ordinary to carry the great name, a criticism which certainly cannot be applied to its successor, the Silver Shadow. The new car was altogether lower and more compact than any of the recent models, in keeping with modern road conditions and the requirements of an owner-driver. This meant that the radiator came down from its considerable height, which it had acquired through the years, to the size and shape that had identified the original Silver Ghost.

The Silver Shadow is a truly modern car, with independent suspension of all 4 wheels, which is self-levelling on the Citröen system. Disc brakes have at last been developed which are dead

The Corniche, the high-performance version of the Rolls-Royce, with a convertible body by Mulliner Park Ward.
This is an adaptation of the steel shell of the Silver Shadow.

silent, hot or cold, the driver's seat is adjusted electrically in all directions, there is power-assisted steering, and even the gear selector is an electric switch. Air conditioning is standard, as is the ultimate in radio and stereo tape equipment.

The Silver Shadow has a combined steel chassis and body, which means that there is no separate frame for coachbuilt bodies. However, Rolls-Royce have acquired two great coachbuilding firms, H.J. Mulliner and Park Ward, who have devised means of altering the standard monocoque so that it can be used as the basis of 2-door and even convertible bodies. At Willesden in North London, where these 2 famous coachbuilders have been combined, cars are built to superb standards quite regardless of price. One almost expects to see King Edward VII or the Czar stroll in to inspect the work; in case they do, a frankly old-fashioned chassis,

ABOVE With the Camargue model, 'the best car in the world' becomes also the most expensive, for the first time.

RIGHT The fashion for two-door prestige cars need not restrict the space for the rear passengers, as the Camargue proves. The use of a small shaft tunnel permits a low floor level but would not be acceptable for a limousine.

the Phantom VI, is still made for limousine or landaulette bodies, fit for state occasions.

The most successful achievement of Mulliner Park Ward is the Camargue. Designed by Pininfarina in Italy but built partly at Willesden and partly at Crewe, the Camargue has the latest 6.7-litre version of the V8 engine and all the Silver Shadow running gear. I have driven every variation of the Shadow as it has developed over the years, but the Camargue has the best steering and roadholding of all of them. The engine may not be quite as silent as the best American V8s, because it is of aluminium rather than cast iron, but it is very quiet indeed. From the exhaust pipe, there is that deep, aristocratic gurgle like a duke's bath water running away.

To drive, the Camargue is one of those very rare cars that simply asks you to go as fast as you dare, or even a bit faster than that; it's much more a driver's car than any of the other post-war models of this make. In looks, it has all the dignity that its famous name implies, plus a crisp, aggressive Italian line. If one begins to feel that the upper-crust car is a thing of the past, the decision of Rolls-Royce to produce the Camargue gives one hope for the future.

The first post-war Daimlers were the medium-sized 6-cylinder models, but a really big car was soon on the stocks; after all, the royal Daimlers must soon be due for replacement. The 5·4-litre straight-eight Daimler was a veritable monster with a 12 ft 3 ins wheelbase, weighing a staggering $57\frac{1}{2}$ cwt. It was also about the most expensive car in the world at that time, the chassis costing £2025, a standard Hooper limousine body £2095, and British purchase tax £2290; of course, a one-off body would cost considerably more.

Hooper built most of the bodies on this chassis and though the 2 firms were separate, Sir Bernard Docker was Chairman of both boards. It is sad to record that Barkers, the famous coachbuilders, had been acquired by Daimler before the war but had been allowed to fade away. Two other great names, Windover and Freestone and Webb, were still operational and built some bodies on the big straight-eights.

The car was conventional, with independent front suspension, and at last the Daimler-Lanchester worm drive had been superseded, a hypoid rear axle taking its place. Only the fluid flywheel and Wilson gearbox remained of all the traditional Daimler features. *Motor* put one of these 7-seaters through its paces, weighing over 3 tons as tested, and the huge vehicle was timed at 82·8 mph, which proves that the engine was certainly developing its claimed 150 bhp.

Few private purchasers could consider such a car but there were still enough foreign potentates to keep up the export quota. Five of these chassis with Hooper bodies, two limousines, two landaulettes, and an open tourer, were ordered for the royal tour of South Africa in 1946. When Princess Elizabeth and Prince Philip went to Australia and New Zealand in 1949, a dozen more were built.

Perhaps the final sunburst of coachbuilding in the grand manner was seen in the Daimlers of Sir Bernard and Lady Docker. For

Sir Bernard and Lady Docker at the Motor Show, with their sumptuous straight-eight Daimler. Though the golden decoration was ostentatious, the craftsmanship of the Hooper body was beyond compare.

several years, these cars were exhibited at the London motor show and as examples of flawless craftsmanship allied with a total disregard of cost, they have probably never been equalled. As Sir Bernard was the Chairman of both Daimler and Hooper, he could get what he wanted, but the standard of the workmanship proved that there were still men who could equal or surpass the best of any era.

It was probably deliberately that this perfection was marred by ostentation and flaunting of wealth. For example, the superb touring limousine at the 1951 show had gold on every piece of brightwork from radiator to tail lights. As if this were not enough, the body was covered with tiny gold stars, while the interior was trimmed with specially woven silk materials containing gold thread. Presumably the object was publicity and that was certainly achieved, the newspapers being full of it, and many people went to the show just to see that one car.

It's hard to imagine how much the 'Docker Daimlers' cost and certainly the firm was in worse financial trouble than usual soon afterwards. Some of the publicity probably did more harm than good and there was a lack of dignity which was possibly noted in official circles. In any case, the Daimler monopoly of royal motors was broken after more than half a century and inevitably the cars from Crewe began to take their place in the Royal Mews.

The last of the Docker Daimlers appeared at the London motor show in 1955. The 1954 car only had silver stars all over it but the last of the line was back on the gold standard. There were no

stars, but ivory was used instead of wood for the gold-framed instrument panel and door cappings. The upholstery was in zebra skin and ivory-coloured leather, the coachwork being finished in ivory white; the 2-door, close-coupled body was on the new 4½-litre 6-cylinder chassis, the straight-eight having been discontinued.

Just after this, the company asked Sir Bernard to resign, which unfortunately resulted in further unwelcome publicity that did untold harm to the famous name. Perhaps the greatest tragedy was that Hooper received mortal wounds, to which they succumbed in 1959; the firm which had made carriages for kings, long before the motoring era, was no more, and it can be said that the art of traditional coachbuilding perished too.

The Daimler Majestic Major v8 was the last of the 'real' Daimlers. Here seen with Lord Brabazon's registration number, it unfortunately arrived too late to carry bodies by the great coachbuilders.

Nevertheless, under the technical direction of Edward Turner, Daimler continued to make excellent cars. In 1958, the Majestic appeared, a very large saloon with an engine of only 3·7 litres that could exceed a genuine 100 mph. Edward Turner, a brilliant engine designer, produced a really modern over-square 4½-litre v8 and the Majestic Major made its bow at the 1959 London show. No book on upper-crust cars would be complete without a mention of this, the last and the best of all the 'real' Daimlers. I had a memorable trip to Le Mans in one, which cornered like a sports car and achieved 122 mph down the Mulsanne straight. It was remarkably light for its size and had none of the ponderous unwieldiness of earlier big Daimlers. A limousine version, carrying a much extended body, was also made with a wheelbase no less than 2 feet longer, and even this was timed at a rousing 113·5 mph.

It was all too late, for although the Majestic Major had a separate chassis, there were no longer any great coachbuilders who could clothe it with their artistic triumphs; the standard bodies were adequate and that was all. Inevitably, Daimler had fallen upon hard times and had been absorbed by Jaguar. The Majestic Major was phased out and thereafter Daimlers were to Jaguars as Bentleys were to Rolls-Royces. Scarcely noticed, the illustrious name of Lanchester had sunk into oblivion during the decline and fall.

Let us not go too closely into the antecedents of the Jaguar. The ss1, with its long bonnet covering a cowering, timorous side-valve Standard engine, was hardly mentioned in polite society. Yet, in an incredibly short time, Bill (later Sir William) Lyons had taken over Le Mans as W.O. Bentley had before him. Jaguar cars brought high performance and luxury into the medium-priced market and, more recently, the 12-cylinder Jaguar – also sold in Double-Six Daimler form – has become a very strong contender in the upper-crust area. The 5·3-litre v12 engine has one chain-driven overhead-camshaft per bank and is outstandingly smooth and quiet throughout its very wide range of revolutions. The car has independent suspension of all 4 wheels but, at the time of writing, no self-levelling system to compensate for different loads is fitted.

The Jaguar is faster than the Rolls, but as both cars have more speed than can generally be used without danger to the driving licence, this is not important. Both cars steer well, though the Rolls-Royce transmits more information from the road surface; the automatic transmission of the Jaguar perhaps lacks smoothness in its changes. Where the Rolls-Royce scores, however, is in better quality control, the Jaguar suffering more teething troubles, as I know from my own experiences and those of friends and correspondents.

At last Mercedes-Benz have returned to the upper crust. Their big 600 has been an excellent car for quite a few years, with its 6·2-litre fuel-injection v8 engine and its pneumatic suspension. Only its brash, Teutonic appearance and excessive display of brightwork has hindered its acceptance as an upper-crust car. Now,

the 450 series, with its 4·5-litre v8 engine and three alternative wheelbase lengths, is making a very serious challenge. More attractive in appearance than the bigger machine, it has plenty of performance though it is not quite as smooth as the Jaguar. Personally, I do not think it handles as well as the other 2, but this may well be altered in later models. I am so glad to see this make climbing towards the top again, after all these years, for no car has a longer history behind it.

Somehow, I seem to have reached the last chapter without giving a watertight definition of an upper-crust car. Perhaps I should not have written so much of cars with large and luxurious bodies. Is the

The Jaguar v12, which is also a Double-Six Daimler with a different radiator grille, is a luxurious car with almost racing performance that costs less than any of its rivals.

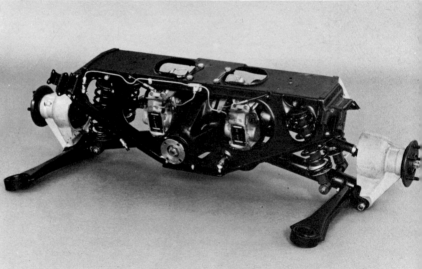

ABOVE The immensely potent 12-cylinder 5·3-litre engine used in Jaguars and Daimlers, here seen in fuel-injection form.
BELOW The independent rear suspension of all Jaguar and Daimler models. Such systems as this have replaced the live axle on nearly every upper-crust car.

OVERLEAF Mercedes-Benz have at last returned to the upper-crust market which their forbears dominated. A 450 SEL.

The Ferrari Berlinetta Boxer, a car of almost unimaginable performance but which is probably the last of the ultra-high speed machines.

OPPOSITE Upper-crust cars of the future must not squander precious fuel. This Citroën has a relatively small engine but achieves high speeds by its advanced aerodynamic shape.

upper-crust car really something as near as possible to a thorough-bred racing car – *le pur sang*, as Ettore Bugatti used to say?

Perhaps I ought to be writing of the Ferrari Berlinetta Boxer, with its centrally-mounted flat-12 engine, 2 seats with little luggage space, and 189 mph maximum speed.

Such cars are marvellous to drive while your licence lasts, but they are so far from being practical under present conditions that their production is unlikely to continue. Very large or thirsty cars may even make their owners unpopular in a world that is short of oil. The upper-crust car of the future could well have an engine of less than 2·5-litres capacity. Perhaps it will be something like the Citröen CX, which has some refinements, such as self-adjusting lights which move with the steering, which even the most expensive cars don't have. One thing is certain; whatever laws and restrictions hamper the enjoyment of motor cars, some way will be found of making a few of them just a little better than all the others. There will always be men who must have the best and others whose need is to create a masterpiece.

Acknowledgments

I would like to thank all those who helped me to write this book and particularly:

My wife, for much hard work and encouragement and for keeping my glass filled.

J.C. Denne, for technical advice on Packards and for letting me crawl all over his cars and photograph them.

Chris Jaques, for providing a beautiful Delaunay-Belleville when I had despaired of finding one in original condition, even in France.

Serge Pozzoli, for giving the Frenchman's point of view on the Delaunay versus Rolls controversy.

Michael Sedgwick, for the loan of valuable documents from his archives.

Peter Hampton, for his help over Rolls-Royce London Edinburgh and 12-cylinder Hispano-Suiza pictures.

Peter Agg, for photographs of an impeccably restored 8-litre Bentley.

List of Illustrations

Index

ROLLS ROYCE

THE BEST SIX-CYLINDER CAR IN THE WORLD?

A FEW REASONS WHY THE ROLLS - ROYCE IS THE BEST SIX - CYLINDER CAR IN THE WORLD.

Because of its

(1) Flexibility.
(2) Lightness and cheapness in tyres.
(3) Reliability.
(4) Silence.
(5) Efficiency and cheapness in upkeep.
(6) Safety—brakes, steering gear, etc.
(7) Ease of manipulation, lightness of steering, clutch operation, etc.

A private owner of a R.R. writes :

"I may say my car is a perfect dream. It is so reliable that I have done away with my carriages and horses."

The original of this letter and many other letters from private owners of Rolls Royce cars may be seen at

ROLLS-ROYCE, Ltd.,

14 & 15, CONDUIT STREET, LONDON, W.

Telegrams : "Rolhead, London."

Telephones : 1497 } Gerrard. 1498

AGENTS for LEICESTER, NOTTINGHAM, RUTLAND, AND DERBYSHIRE.. .. ..
AGENTS for NORTH RIDING OF YORKSHIRE AND DURHAM .. ..
AGENTS, FRANCE .. ..
AGENTS, UNITED STATES of AMERICA ..
AGENTS, OTTAWA (CANADA) and DISTRICT .. .. ..

The Midland Counties Motor Garage Co., Granby Street, Leices..

The Cleveland Car Co., Cleveland Bridge Works, Darlington.
La Société Anonyme " L'Eclaire," 59, Rue la Boëtié, Paris.
The Rolls-Royce Import Co.. Broadway New York.
Messrs. Ketchum & Co.. corner of Bank St. and Sparks St., Ottawa.